TRANSFORMATIONAL INTELLIGENCE:
Creating Cultures of Honor @ Home and Work

Lifeforming Institute

101 N. Lynnhaven Rd. Suite 102
Virginia Beach, Virginia 23452
Printed in the United States of America on acid-free paper.

ISBN-978-0-9914824-0-5

I

**Transformational Intelligence: Creating Cultures of Honor @
Home and Work**

Designed by Jana Rade, design@americanbookpublishing.com

Library of Congress Cataloging-in-Publication Data available upon request.

TRANSFORMATIONAL INTELLIGENCE:
Creating Cultures of Honor @ Home and Work

Joseph L. Umidi

TABLE OF CONTENTS

INTRODUCTION

Transformation is another word that is on the best-seller list, but has come to mean just about anything. It differs from transaction for it is not primarily about the exchange of information, but a marriage of that information with the power of sustainable motivation. More than an experience that could be described as common inspiration, transformation, like the caterpillar to the butterfly, is closer to illumination. It is an inner awakening that happens from the inside out, not the outside in.

At Life-forming Leadership Coaching, we have been watching real transformation happen through our training and coaching process around the world over the last sixteen years in almost every possible scenario. These include the poor, rich, male, female, youth, elderly, literate, illiterate, Asian, Latin, African, European, Caribbean, and more. We have hundreds of stories from thousands of fulfilled coaches, clients, and organizations. This book is a key to why such phenomena may become a movement. More importantly, it may be the breakthrough for you, as you desire to see your dreams fulfilled at home and work.

A key reason for this possibility is the fundamental philosophy of the extravagant worth of every individual, that is rooted in a healthy theology of the authentic, relational, and organic Christian message. This message and motivation is that God is for us, not against us, and we have an opportunity and mandate to fulfill our unique design and destiny. Part of that purpose is to be modeled in the home and workplace environments, the places where real transformation meets the real world. This book does that without being religious. Like God, it is for you, not for its own agenda.

Whether you are a burning flame of faith or a burned-out statistic of faithless religion, this book can revive you and the organization where you are spending the best hours of your day serving. It is a book that moves transformation beyond a personal experience to a culture shift. It does so intentionally and with intensity by taking your intelligence more seriously than has probably been the case at this point in your life and calling. Thus, its success will be measured by those who live and work with you regularly.

It is our goal that you experience validation in the reading and application of these chapters. We envision schools, businesses, organizations, and churches using this for their staff and personnel in ways that will make these entities go from good to great. Those of us who have labored with little remuneration over the years to serve the global community with these principles are audacious enough to believe that this book can even impact a nation by the systematic application of these truths to the key vocations which shape the culture of that nation. Only time will tell. Our first hope is that the time you take to reflect and apply the following chapters will alter your life just enough to make the daily difference where it counts: at home and work.

Dr. Joseph Umidi, January 2014

CHAPTER ONE
CULTURES OF HONOR

Culture Shift

Culture[1] affects everyone, everywhere, every day. Some of it is in our face, like the ads for erectile dysfunction that embarrass everyone during the few family times we gather around the same channel anymore. Most of it is subtle and

---

[1]Culture is "**a** : the integrated pattern of human knowledge, belief, and behavior that depends upon the capacity for learning and transmitting knowledge to succeeding generations; **b** : the customary beliefs, social forms, and material traits of a racial, religious, or social group; *also* : the characteristic features of everyday existence (as diversions or a way of life shared by people in a place or time); **c** : the set of shared attitudes, values, goals, and practices that characterizes an institution or organization like a corporate culture focused on the bottom line; **d** : the set of values, conventions, or social practices associated with a particular field, activity, or societal characteristic." (*Merriam Webster Dictionary*, 2009).

soothing, like the background noise of the waves as we doze off on the beach. All of it counts for who we are and what we become. The purpose of this chapter is to lay a foundation to transform whatever culture we are facing and shift it into a culture that honors people and purposes, especially those that are near and dear to us.

All cultures contain positive and negative aspects, and it is incumbent upon all of us to not limit ourselves to the acceptable "dumb-down" standard of tolerance today, meaning we accept everything from another culture simply because it is another culture. The pendulum swing from a mono-cultural to a multicultural focus over the past decades, in which we have become so enamored by any other different culture, has missed the point. Our real call is to create culture, not simply to worship culture or become a creature of culture. Every family, company, church, and community group is a candidate to model a creative approach to culture that maximizes the best in people and the potential of the culture to contribute to the uplifting of the community and city. That maximization will require an intentional focus in our approach to transform the role of culture in our lives.

My wife has spent the last twenty years researching the cultures of groups in remote parts of the globe in order to understand their oral traditions and how they communicate their values through "non-printed" methods, such as story, dance, and music. This has taken her to remote locations in Nepal, Thailand, Siberia, India, Indonesia, and other countries to discover how to serve them in creating culture for themselves that will enable their children to avoid the contagion of the HIV/aids virus, sex slave trade, and rites that marginalize women or the handicapped. Her goal, and my goal in this chapter, is to encourage you to create a culture of honor in the cultures that most shape our lives and future: the home and workplace.

Key to this culture shift is the role of values that are the foundation of cultures. The premise of this book is that we can upgrade our values [2] to promote honor at the top of the list and become intentional as to how to implement it at home and work. Relationships are at the core of any culture and the way we honor others in those relationships is critical to the depth and meaning of those relationships in family, community, and workplace. Whether it is the Gobi desert in Mongolia or the suburbs of Arizona, the gift of honor [3] can transform a relationship and those relationships can shift a culture to be an environment that brings out the best in us and through us.

Gifts of Honor

When was the last time your family honored one another? Was it the culturally accepted version only of birthday, anniversary, Mother's Day, Father's Day, and, of course, Christmas? How does your work environment show honor? Is it only the twenty-year gold watch, employee of the month gift certificate, and the long lost bonus? These are the minimums to be part of the culture, but they do not motivate the maximums that can transform the culture. We need an

---

[2]There are various tools to prioritize life values that effective coaches use to help people move from aspirations to actual value-based living. Contact www.lifeformingcoach.com.

[3]See the foundational work on this topic, *The Gift of Honor,* by Gary Smalley and John Trent (Nashville: Thomas Nelson, 1987).

upgrade of relational honor, a download of transformational behaviors that will result in significance, productivity, loyalty, camaraderie, unity, identity, courage, and tenacity at home and work. In short, we need our home and work environments to become cultures of honor.[4]

So what is this honor we are describing? Honor is a relational or social term that identifies how people in any society evaluate one another. How we evaluate one's worth affects our attitude and behavior towards that person. That is why at the root of most cultures there is an expression of giving honor to God through ways that represent worth. The Hebrew word "kabod" means "weighty"[5] or to give weight to someone. It is a word that grants respect, value, importance, and even authority in our lives. It is translated "glory" in English and is the primary call to give God glory or honor as the first priority in our lives that enable us to then have a lifestyle of giving honor to others throughout our lives.

John was at a yard sale and saw a tarp over what looked like a bike. He pulled back the tarp and underneath was a beat up old Harley Davidson motorcycle. The tires were flat and the metal was all rusted out. John asked if the bike was for sale and the owner said, "Make me an offer." John said, "How about $35?" He heard the quick reply, "Get it out of here, it is yours!"

---

[4]The author first heard this term at Bethel Church in Redding, California, in its unique role in training men and women to create less religious and more authentic and dynamic kingdom of God cultures in their communities. The application of that here is to the home and workplace.

[5]Lawrence O. Richards, *Expository Dictionary of Bible Words* (D.C.: Regency, 1985), 310.

A few weeks later John decided to see if he could still get some parts that were missing on the bike. When he called the Harley Davidson company, the service rep said, "I'll need the serial number," so he scraped off the rust to find it and repeated it to him. The service rep replied, "Can you give me that number again?" When John repeated it, there was a long pause on the other side of the phone before the rep finally told him he will have to call him back. An hour later the owner called and said, "Sight unseen I'll give you $100,000 for the bike. It was specially made for Elvis and we have been looking for that bike for a long time."[6]

The worth of the bike was determined by who it was made for. You, your family members, and work associates are made for the honor and glory of God. With that cornerstone in place we can build a foundation for a culture of honor at home and work.

Value, respect, esteem, regard, worth, and significance all flow out of the refreshing fountain of honor. Yet what leaks out from the septic tank of dishonor is disgrace, shame, humiliation, scorn, and contempt. It devalues someone to the point that dictionaries even refer to dishonor as "rape." One of the most common ways we dishonor is to disregard God or people. Treating another as only part of a blurred landscape of our lives, ordinary, common, unimportant, even taken for granted, is to discount them and their unique purpose. Honor requires celebration and validation, not comfort zone toleration.

Sounds of Honor

---

[6]Seminar presentation by Brent Lucy (Chesapeake, Virginia New Life Western Branch, 2009).

Have you ever felt like saying, "Are you even listening to me?" That anger you feel inside comes from a sense of not being valued as a person, what you have to say is not relevant, and your needs are not seen as important. It is basic to human dignity that we are listened to and someone pays attention to us. There is a "sound" of dishonor that could be the sound of silence when we don't speak up for another or the sound of emptiness when we do not seize the opportunity to validate another. Sometimes the sound of dishonor is in criticism, judgment, tone of voice, or body language.[7]

I will never forget the conflict intervention I attempted early in my career without knowing how to set ground rules for a successful interaction. With a high profile leader and a mid-level staffer sitting in front of me, I attempted to have them work out their issues. Somewhere in the heat of the exchange, the leader just got up and left the room; too busy and too preoccupied to spend anymore of her valuable time with such a subordinate's issues. The devastation and demoralization was profound and reinforced the hierarchical culture of dishonor that had been ingrained in the organization for years. It made me determined, on my watch, to find a more excellent way to shift the work culture, and has culminated in the following chapters that address these kinds of toxic scenarios.

The sounds of honor are much different. They are words of high value and words of a hopeful future. They edify or build people up and make them feel singularly prized and special. They impart strength and courage and enable people

---

[7]See Real Talk Training seminar materials described in www.lifeformingcoach.com.

14

to get to the finish line through tough projects, circumstances beyond control, suffering, and setbacks. In business culture, it is sometimes referred to as the power of gratitude or affirmation.[8]   In the family culture, it has been known as the power of the "blessing."[9]

Something amazing happens when parents intentionally look for opportunities through the week to speak positive and powerful word pictures that capture the imagination of their children and help them to see themselves as they really are, and what they can fully become. Words at the dinner table, tender moment words at "tuck-in time," and well-chosen words at key teachable moments create a culture of honor that is actually the gift of honor to our children and grandchildren. In this atmosphere, children learn to honor their parents and parents to honor their children and treat them with care and consideration. Marriage is sustained as much by mutual respect and honor as by physical intimacy and affection. Women are to be honored, not abused, and employees are to be treated with dignity and compassion.

Stories of Honor

Rural Canada

---

[8]See the excellent business books by Ken Blanchard, *The One Minute Manager* and *Raving Fans: A Revolutionary Approach to Customer Service* (New York: William Morrow & Co., 1993).

[9]*The Blessing* by Gary Smalley and John Trent (New York: Pocket Books, 1986) emphasizes the home being a place of "meaningful touch, spoken messages, attaching high value, picturing a special future, and activating a regular commitment" to our children.

I worked for seven years in a small Canadian city with an honor deficit in the stories of people who gave meaning to their culture. From the very foundation of their town there was a major injustice that created a culture of dishonor and was still affecting two groups hundreds of years later. Two cultures and language groups occupied this city in almost a 50/50 ratio but the stories of noncooperation, distrust, prejudice, and stereotypes were deeply ingrained in the psyche of the people. It was evident to an outsider that they had come to accept living in this murky fish tank as if it was normal and it is all they could ever expect.

After being captivated by the stories in Alex Haley's classic, *"Roots,"* I teamed up with some leaders to determine how we could shift the culture to one of more honor. We invited all the elderly who had been in the community, with their own roots for generations, to find some of the oldest pictures and artifacts from their family and come to a community hall we rented for a Saturday "Roots Day." With almost 200 card tables set up with fine linen, they saw each of the items that told the stories of the past as we filled the hall with the lineage of the community's "pioneers." In addition, we marketed to the entire community to come and visit them on this day, and hear the stories of the people who had dreamed and sacrificed to make this community viable.

Something transformational and sustainable happened that day. The elderly received the gift of honor from us and, more importantly, from the community residents who had no idea of the past and how it affected the present. Conversations went to a meaningful level, talking of dreams realized and yet to be fulfilled. In this multi-generational and multicultural moment in time, something shifted in the way people viewed each other, moving towards a visible respect and reverence.

From that moment on, we gained a momentum that enabled us to build a model of community transformation that included the businesses and local government for years to come.

Washington, D.C.

In a more recent past, I had the privilege of meeting an ambassador from Israel at a public lecture attended by VIPs from various backgrounds. I escorted my wife who sang and carried her heavy keyboard. Because I was her transportation I was invited back to the VIPs after the event that was attended by invitation only. Somehow the ambassador singled me out and engaged me in an eight-minute conversation that was extraordinary. Though we were not totally in agreement on his points, it was a powerful conversation that I remember to this day. It seemed as if I was the honored guest, and my perspective was sought after and taken as seriously as if I were his boss, the prime minister.

I asked my wife on the way home, "What school does an ambassador go to? I think I need to go there and get what he has."

Four years later my wife was asked to sing again at an event in the Capitol of our nation that was the goodbye celebration for this gentleman, as he was to return home to a new government post. This time I was to both wear a tuxedo and carry the keyboard. I tried to find a way to be excused because I did not want to attend a politically charged meeting, attended by the former Republican leader of the House of Representatives and the present Democratic leader in charge, along with the 500 guests from all the religious, cultural, and political differences you could gather in one room. I was prepared for the political spin, hype, and posturing that could make for a long evening in a less-than-comfortable attire.

Sometime during the event, I realized that this was not at all what I expected. The atmosphere was drenched with humility, honor, celebration, and even a sense of family unity around this couple's four-year tenure representing his country to us. As I conversed with the guests at our table, I discovered the key reason. Each of the guests at my table had an extraordinary conversation with the ambassador that had impacted them, similar to what I had experienced, even if it was only a brief exchange. The final confirmation came when I heard the stories from the platform personalities that basically repeated my experience to the letter. Over 500 people from every walk of life had been transformed by a conversation with the ambassador. Now they were able to shift the culture of the most politically polarizing part of our country in a meeting, and in their lives, because someone had given them the gift of honor in a relational exchange that was transformational.

A key to both of these stories is a return to a child-like curiosity about life and people that genuinely wants to know and discover, without having an agenda. A transformational coaching approach that is a vehicle for this curiosity is first, to discover how someone is a uniquely designed individual according to his or her personality and temperament. There are many effective assessments that explore such design. Second, there are also the unique desires that drive people with energy and passion, mostly discovered in clarifying core values. Third, to understand the unique dreams that have captured someone's imagination over the years. All of this can help uncover one's unique destiny. Fourth, emphasis that gives them their tailor-made mission and results in their

18

unique legacy. In family and working relationships that honor these in attitudes, behaviors, and conversations, we will create cultures that honor and have a distinctiveness about them that brings out the best in people and organizations.

Each of us is a story that is being told about family, work, health, friends, and happiness.

Each of us contributes to the story being told by the organizations where we invest both our time and talents.[10] The challenge for many of us is that we may not be living our own story but the indoctrinated story of our culture that has held us captive to its own voice and values. This book is an attempt to help you get in touch with your "tailor-made" story. It honors you by having faith in you for the spiritual integrity that only you can steward to rescript your future to become a person of honor. Your story of honor is what you can do with the following materials applied personally. Your legacy is what you do with the culture of honor you shift and create by influencing others through the seven categories of transformational intelligences.

---

[10]See chapters one and four of the excellent book, *The Power of Story* by Jim Loehr (New York: Free Press, 2007).

CHAPTER TWO
HONORING YOUR UNIQUE
"INTELLIGENCE"

"How intelligent are you?"

Most of you reading this will place yourselves at a six - seven level on a scale of one - ten, at least when asked in public. The problem is that this is not the right question for success at home or work. In these unprecedented economic times we need another way of asking this if we are to have sustainable significance in our work and productive influence through our work. We need another way of defining intelligence. We need to honor another set of criteria for redefining success in our lives.

One of the creators of the IQ test, Alfred Binet, would be shocked to see the way we have now interpreted it in our cultures, including the infamous SAT. He never intended it to measure "mental worth" or the thinking that a person could not become more intelligent over time with a development plan to do so.[11] The dark side of the eugenics movement and the passage of involuntary sterilization came out of those revisionists, like Lewis Terman in 1916, who took this approach to measuring intelligence where its founders never intended it to go.

The problem with the SAT approach to intelligence is that it is only going after one kind of intelligence. It has failed to take into account other types and, therefore, has no way of assessing and measuring their development. We need another approach that starts with another question:

"How are you intelligent?"

In this introduction, we acknowledge that this issue of intelligence theory had been around for a while and has various approaches. There is an excellent book called, *The Frames of Mind: The Theory of Multiple Intelligences* by Howard Gardner from Harvard, written twenty years ago.[12] Gardner's seven intelligences are different from our seven "intels" given in this book, but they are well worth noting in the following brief overview.

Gardner theorizes that his <u>linguistic intelligence</u> is the ability to communicate, to be able to put words together, and to think linearly, logically, and mathematically. These

---

[11]Ken Robinson, *The Element: How Finding Your Passion Changes Everything* (New York: Penguin Group, 2009), 38ff.

[12]Howard Gardner, *The Frames of Mind: The Theory of Multiple Intelligences* (New York: Basic Books, 2004). This twentieth anniversary edition has some excellent responses to criticism of the multiple intelligence theory and more bad news on the ongoing fallout from standard intelligent testing on our children in their development.

concepts are usually what we look at in our educational system as describing the typical "A" student. In our educational models, we are mostly looking for intelligence in two areas: linguistic and logical mathematical. That is the traditional educational focus on what some people call the left-brain---the side of us that is measured in some of the core IQ tests to measure our intelligence.

Gardner goes on to talk about other intelligences. He calls one a <u>musical intelligence</u>. This is not simply the ability to play an instrument but the ability to understand how things fit together in harmony, how things resonate, or how things appear or sound. We would not necessarily measure that intelligence by how we play an instrument but how we actually approach a problem, framing it in a way that mirrors the way a music conductor would approach the orchestra.

Gardner describes another intelligence as a <u>spatial intelligence</u>, which is recognizing ways, connecting things, or relating visually. Certainly artists may have this in their ability to sculpt or to paint. Both the musical and the spatial are particularly aspects of right-brain processes so people can be highly intelligent in those areas. There are powerful stories coming from people who did not fit into the traditional educational model of sitting and listening to lectures, but came alive when they discovered their musical intelligence or their spatial intelligence. That new enthusiasm was not only evidenced in those areas, but also in the ability to do well in the more linguistic or logical mathematical sides since they now paid more attention to all of the learning process.

Gardner mentions the <u>bodily kinesthetic intelligence</u>, which is the ability to learn by doing or the "concreteness" of being active in the learning process. This is intelligence in understanding balance, the ability to arrange our physical world, or to be physical in the sense of appreciating our physical environment. There are many ways that can be expressed, which we will defer for some other writing.

Gardner concludes with the interpersonal intelligence and the intrapersonal intelligence, saying that both of these would come more in the subconscious area. This would not be either right-brain or left-brain areas, but under the surface on how we interpret things or feel about things. Interpersonal and communication skills, the ability for people to resonate, certainly can be learned, but those having this intelligence have unique "radar" for others.

Our musical "intel" also requires perhaps a bodily kinesthetic intelligence to be able to play an instrument, but it also could require an interpersonal intelligence in conducting the relational harmony of an orchestra who play the instruments as well. Maybe we are not in a media vocation, but we have this "intel" of something musical about us so we can focus on having crescendos, or tones, or harmonies in the way we are presenting a product or a process by applying this musical "intel" in the advertising field.

When we hear these intelligences described from the academic world, our first response may be that these are the same as inborn learning styles, or are simply connected only to certain vocations that one is pursuing. In this introductory summary, we are saying that these "intels" or these intelligences, are not just an IQ that we inherit. The genius of the frames of mind research by Dr. Gardner is that there is a plurality of intelligences that we can have, each with its own strengths and constraints. "Intels" are not set in stone from birth, but can be increased by our environments and by the resources that we put into developing them.

24

Now that is exciting because no matter what vocational "mountain" we are called to scale, we can increase our intelligence to influence those mountains as part of our own legacy and life purpose. The transformational intelligences we will be talking about are actually different than Gardner's list, but they also result in honoring the unique way we express ourselves intelligently. Knowing this, we can put ourselves in an environment to develop and stretch these, and to challenge these in healthy ways. In essence, we can create a culture of honor at home and work by honoring and activating the way our spouse, children, and employees are able to express their unique intelligence.

In the past we did not have much vocabulary for these things. Somebody was either bright or dull. We just called them intelligent. We simply said these are smart people. We might say, "Well, Thomas Jefferson or Fredrick Douglas or Mahatma Gandhi, they are just smart people." But it is really not about IQ only. Intelligence, as described by Dr. Gardner, and as I will describe in the transformational intelligences, are ways to define how we approach tasks and disciplines in different domains. In different aspects of our job, whether we may approach them musically, spatially, or linguistically, we will utilize a tailor-made coaching approach that both honors unique design in us and the ability to adjust and develop that in others.

The other question that we have regarding these intelligences is, how do we measure our "intelligence?" Beginning with our own personal assessment we can begin to target increasing our perspective on their improvement. We can research where we have the best opportunity to develop and express our intelligence. We can pursue the kind of training to be successful according to our "intelligence" and vocational calling. The key as we introduce these seven transformational intelligences is how to make us more effective at work.

For many of us who are just getting by, just showing up, just putting in our time by punching the clock, we sense that we are underdeveloped, underutilized, and underpaid. We can no longer play it safe nor can we afford to be in an environment that just wants to coast. We need to place ourselves at different points in our lives and in our vocations in an environment that engages and stretches us. We learn more from "stretching mistakes" coupled with feedback and debriefing than we ever will with just a posture of risk avoidance. The best way to develop our intelligences is to be with people in the environment that sharpens one another. We can summarize the implications of this introduction with these key questions:

"Where will you find the courage to change your environment to one that can 'excel your intel'?"

"What needs to change in you first in order to make your environment conducive to your 'full intel' expression?"

We want you to know from this point forward, our team at Life-forming Leadership Coaching, with its training for "7M coaching," is ready to take you to the next level because the coaching relationship is your best source of courage. Courageous conversations that engage, stretch, and enable you to develop your "intels" are what are needed in today's economic environment. We recognize that the whole process of learning is one that puts us in places to do the behavioral change we desire. As you study and access the seven wheels of transformational intelligences, be prepared for a conversation with a peer or a coach that will maximize your ability to either change yourself or your environment to be where you need to be.

How to Maximize the Seven "Intels" Wheels Assessment

The 7M "intels" will help you redefine brilliance for creating a culture of honor at home and at work. These are core intelligences that will enable you to ascend your vocational mountain, to scale areas that have been treacherous, and to reach the summits of sustainable peak performance. Those phrases are packed with lots of promises. We do not want to over promise and under deliver with rhetoric. What we want is for you to pay attention to more than just what is required to be excellent in your career, vocation, or profession, either in terms of degrees or the tools of the trade. Beyond that is the need to acquire the ability to be able to express yourself in ways that connect with people, connect with purpose, and enable you to be a principled man or woman who is promotable, and who has the kind of moral and ethical life that people will admire.

INSTRUCTIONS

"Assessments are only as effective as the level of discussion they generate."

This quote is only to encourage you to dialogue with a peer, a coach, or a trainer on how you can get the most out of any attempt to look at yourself. Our patterns of perceiving and interpreting what we see have both strengths and weaknesses that can only be dealt with in a safe dialogue with those interested in our development.

Each of the wheels is divided into categories, which are further divided into sections or "spokes" of the wheel. Each of these categories and spokes are described in detail in the following chapters to give you a common ground from which to begin.

The goal of this assessment is first to understand the role of each descriptor in the context of your vocational life. Many of these will also apply to your family context as well as work.

Every vocation/career requires its own benchmarks for entry and advancement, including education, certifications, milestone achievements, etc. However, it is the author's contention that the unique role of these "intelligences" will be more important in the present economic era for both significance and success in one's occupation than has been the case in the past.

PERSONAL USE

For personal use each wheel can be used to measure your present level of competency as it relates to how these competencies are impacting your work world. Each spoke begins at the hub at "zero" and moves to the rim of the wheel at "ten." Nine to ten represents your having maximal level all the time at this particular competency, six to eight represents above average competency most of the time, five represents medium competency most of the time, two to four represents minimal competency most of the time, and zero to one represents no competency most of the time.

OTHER USE (coach, supervisor, peer, 360[13])

For helpful feedback by another, each person would measure your level of competency in the context that they see you or interact with you from their perspective. While some of these may not lend themselves to being measured by another, the ability to determine whether these exist through the eyes of another can be insightful. The real benefit from this is to compare major discrepancies between the personal and other assessment and then to discuss how these may relate to "blind spots" or perhaps, to the unique environment of the work culture that may itself contribute to these discrepancies. Of course, anyone who uses these assessment wheels will need to read and reflect on the descriptive materials in order to have any value in the role of these assessments.

ASSESSMENT ACTION STEPS

Every assessment is an opportunity for a focused attention to make a helpful change. One key way is a series of action steps that have S.M.A.R.T. goals (specific, measurable, achievable, realistic, and timely). Here are some recommendations:

---

[13]See Susan Scott, *Fierce Conversations: Achieving Success at Work and in Life One Conversation at a Time* (New York: Penguin Group, 2004), 38-59 for the difference between 360 degrees anonymous assessment and 365 days authentic feedback.

(1). Establish goals in any area in which you are motivated to take action over a ninety-day period. Determine the difference this ninety-day focus has made in your job significance, productivity, and/or feedback from others on your influence in the workplace.

(2). Find a peer, who will also assess himself or herself, and establish his or her own goals for improvement. Provide weekly support, encouragement, and accountability (S.E.A.) with a phone call on progress and roadblocks during the ninety-day period.

(3). Engage a coach who will help you articulate and record these goals and put them in a tailor-made personal growth plan that targets beyond the ninety-day time frame.

(4). Establish a small group "intel" team who will rotate presenting roles in providing further input and resources at regular meetings, along with updates on personal progress and group consultation on overcoming roadblocks.

(5). Become a seven mountains coach who can use these "intels" to help others. (See www.lifeformingcoach.com)

CHAPTER THREE
SPIRITUAL INTELLIGENCE

Spiritual Wheel   SQ
Transformational Intelligences for Home and Work©

SPIRITUAL INTELLIGENCE – SQ

"So what makes a person spiritual, and what difference does that make at work?" That is the first question I encounter whenever I mention this topic to executives. It is a question that is well worth the time it will take to read this chapter for a unique frame of reference.

There are as many definitions to spirituality as there are to religions, I am sure. With the unique SQ approach being presented, there is an ability to redefine and reframe this perspective. God's relationship with us, our integration with ourselves, our ability to live that out with our family; and then expressing that on the job, brings a fresh approach to this topic. These are areas that everyone can relate to despite their particular religious tradition. It is an integration that people are longing to see, no matter what religious traditions or

Joseph L. Umidi

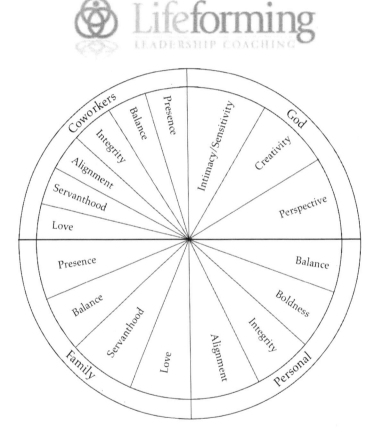

expressions we adhere to because people prefer that we be real and not religious, no matter how much devotion we may have in a particular expression. At the end of the day, people only want to know how real we are with ourselves, with our family, and with the people we work with.

That is the litmus test for a spiritual quotient in the vocational mountains. Spiritually intelligent men and women create a culture of honor in the workplace.

We should start with first things first and that is what we are calling spiritual intelligence or the spiritual quotient in our lives. This SI or SQ is not about being religious. It is not about being denominational. It is really about being what we already are. We are spiritual beings with the capability to increase our SQ in ways that make the difference.

I remember a wake-up call when one individual described his research that he did with CEOs, asking the question, "When was the first time you can remember that you actually saw yourself in your mind doing what you are doing today?" Almost 70 percent said it was in fourth grade.[14] It seems that we all have had a glimpse of our destiny or purpose in early awakenings. We have a sense of the reason why we are here, or at least what gives us meaning as to why we are here, early on. God has a continuous daily practice of speaking to us and through us in many different ways, both in and outside of our houses of worship.

Without any particular religion, denominational background, or training, we can remember insights we have received "on-site" at special places along our callings and

---

[14]See Bob Biehl's resources for his video tape presentation, called "Fourth Grade."

career, whether it is in a retreat or in the shower. This is what
we are talking about in the spiritual quotient.

SQ is really essential and the most fundamental of all the
intelligences since it is the source of guidance for us
throughout our life. One way to define this SQ would be in
the language of our drive for meaning and connection with
God. This spiritual quotient is the true north on our moral,
ethical, and principle compass. Whenever it seems like "this is
the way, this is the right way," wherever and whenever that
comes from, we all have had that awakening from our
spiritual slumber. The good news is we can have it daily.

In the Bible, in Proverbs 20:27, it says, "The spirit of man
is the candle of the Lord." All of us then, as spiritual beings,
have the potential in God's design to be "bright" or
"brilliant" and can have a light that shines in us and through
us at home and at work. The authors Dana Zohar and Ian
Marshall put it like this: "I am like IQ which computers have
and EQ which exists in higher mammals. SQ, spiritual
quotient, is uniquely human and the most fundamental of the
three. The spiritual quotient is what we use to develop our
longing and capacity for meaning, vision, and value. It allows
us to dream. It is in essence what makes us human."[15]

I love that phrase on dreaming. SQ gives us permission to
dream or even dream again. I have come to see over thirteen
years of coach training around the world that the pathway to
transformation comes through our lifelong dreams.[16] Re-
awakening and reconnecting to our dreams will cause us to be
excited before our feet hit the ground when we get out of bed

[15]Danah Zohr and Ian Marshall, *Spiritual Quotient: Connecting
with Our Spiritual Intelligence* (Bloomsbury, 2001).
[16]See Michael Johnson's Web site at www.withreach.com.

in the morning and we think about our work. Dreams keep us energized, keep us motivated, and keep us looking for the best, even in difficult times.

There is a large international hotel chain, in which I had a coach-training contract, that wanted to be number one in customer service. They had already determined that the best way to do it would be simply to come up with a list of excellent behaviors for their front-line staff and to make sure these workers checked off as many of those as possible each day to reach this goal. In our first manager meeting I suggested to them that in addition to having that list, they could actually come at it from a different angle. I recommended they approach this goal in terms of what most motivated their workers to be creative in serving customers, and emphasized that they first discover the dreams of what their front-line workers had regarding their jobs and why they were there. It was the beginning stage of developing a culture of honor, but it was met with resistance. Most of these managers thought that was kind of odd. They had not operated that way before. Quite frankly, many of these managers looked down on their front-line staff in a condescending attitude. They were not as educated. They certainly did not have the same social and economic background. It created a stir, but they took a chance when they hired me that I was on to something. That is when I gave them their first assignment.

I trained them on how to shift the culture of their supervisory meeting with their staff by asking questions. In the very next staff meeting they were to ask, "When you kick your feet out of bed in the morning, before they hit the ground and you think about coming to work, what excites you the most about working here?" To their surprise they discovered that there was 75 percent of their front-line staff that were motivated because they were fulfilling a dream to send money back home to their relatives, parents, children, and spouses, to be able to help them in the village, and lift them out of their poverty.

Something unusual happened to these managers. First of all, they realized that their dreams for coming to work were not nearly as big as their front-line people. They also realized that their staff had family values that were higher than theirs and a sacrificial living that challenged their own self-centeredness. A subtle shift began in the hotel work atmosphere as we began to move forward. The managers became more than supervisors with a check-off list. They became dream managers helping their people fulfill their own SQ. Today this hotel chain is approaching number one in customer service excellence because they honored the spiritual intelligence of their front-line staff. Even though they are not educated, they had the same longing for meaning, significance, and dream fulfillment as does the most educated of us all.

We are going to present in each of these intelligences what we call a "wheel of assessment." In this chapter you have the SQ or the spiritual intelligence wheel. It has at the hub several spokes that go out to the circumference. The hub represents zero and at the tip of the circumference it represents the number ten. That indicates, as you do a self-assessment, your present level of competency regarding where you are at from zero to ten as you assess each of those spokes on a particular wheel.[17] It can also access, in some cases, a particular level of

---

[17]Refer to the seven "intels" wheels assessment for specific instructions on how to use these wheels.

balance that you feel you have in terms of which spokes you assess at eight or nine or a ten and others in which you are at quite a low number. As we take a look at each of these spokes I will describe them and give you a chance to do some reflection on your own.

You will also notice that on the SQ wheel, there is on the rim four different sections or categories. There is one for God, one for personal, one for family, and one for co-workers. It is important to realize the power of assessment as we talk about creating a culture of honor at work and rediscovering ways to become effective on the job, and to be able to have more of an impact on our vocational mountain.

In this perspective we are redefining success in terms of the influence we have in our seven mountains or the "spheres of influence" we steward in our vocations.[18] In that redefinition of what we mean for us to be successful there must be a congruency at home as well as at work. In other words, we can put in ninety hours a week and be the best worker, leader, manager, or CEO, yet if our family does not have us, or our time, or we are not paying attention to their life issues and transitions, then our ladder has leaned against the wall that may well be the wrong wall at the end of the day.

The assumption that we are bringing into this discussion of scaling the vocational mountains is that at the core of every mountain is a healthy family, even if we are single, and family life are meaningful relationships of those that are close to you, or whether we are a single parent with our own working definition of the family. Those who are looking to us in either that bloodline family or extended family, the key is

---

[18]See www.lancelearning.com for a description of the 7 mountains and Lance Wallnau's 7M University.

that we have a desire to live a life that is successful from the definition of our spouse, our children, our brothers, and our sisters, as well as the people that we are working with during the week.

With that being noted, it is time for us to begin to look at defining this wheel. What do these spokes mean in this <u>God quadrant</u>? First, and most importantly, there is a desire in each of us on this first spoke to have a sense of <u>intimacy or sensitivity</u> to the Creator, to God, personally, that we would have an ability in some way to know that God has uniquely and lovingly created us for a purpose, and that this purpose in us is close to God's heart. However we express this, we are recognizing that many of us, even before we were religious or involved in any particular faith subcultures, had moments where we had awakenings or connections and had a sense of the nearness with God. This is an intimacy and sensitivity in many ways that is beyond just religious talk. It is really about a relationship, a personal relationship with a personal God.[19]

When you think about keys from some of the great leaders in the past, they talk about moments in prison, or moments in deserts, or moments where they just felt closeness and a sense of purpose. Even in the Old Testament stories of Moses that so many faiths look to, whether it is Islam or Judaism or Christianity, there is a description of this SQ. One key passage in Deuteronomy 5:24 and following describes where God is speaking to Moses and then the people are speaking to Moses. The breakthrough came when the people

---

[19]*New York Times* bestseller, *The Shack* by William P. Young (Newbury Park, Ca.: Windblown Media, 2007), though theologically controversial, has motivated many to a new understanding of intimacy with God and is recommended for the reader.

said, "We have heard his voice." That means the people were saying we have heard God's voice ourselves. This was a great breakthrough that everyone can have the SQ of being sensitive and intimate. "We have heard God's voice and we have seen that God can speak with men and can live."

This is an incredible breakthrough in which people realized they have access to God himself and can actually commune with him. Yet, almost immediately, they fell right back into their fearful or religious ways, and they said to Moses in verse 27, "You go near and you hear all that God may say and tell us all what God says to you and then we will hear and do it." The lesson here is that the propensity or tendency for all of us is simply to have a professional religious clergy do all this SQ stuff and we will just let them tell us what God is saying and we will respond to it as we see fit. But that is not the way it is meant to be because God, who is alive and can speak to anyone, anywhere, and anytime, wants to speak to us both on and off the job. In the corresponding passage to this story in the Old Testament, the Bible says in Hebrews, 12:25, to not refuse him who is continually speaking to you.

The spoke of intimacy means we can hear God on the job and in the midst of some difficult circumstances, conflicts, no-win options, double binds, and insurmountable odds. God does a great job of communicating to those that simply desire to listen.[20] The key is to have a sensitivity that is tuned to hearing God.

Most of us want to be more productive at work. The counterintuitive principle that I have learned is that

---

[20]See chapter eight of *You Were Born For This* by Bruce Wilkinson (Colorado Springs: Multmonah Books, 2009) for a practical model.

"productivity is really a byproduct of intimacy." In other words, when I meditate in the morning or when I reflect throughout the day and just pull away and listen with my ear tuned in to that "still small voice" from God, that inner voice, I find that I am more productive throughout the day. I have less paper that I have to crumble after several attempts to do e-mail. I have fewer times that I have to pull my foot out of my mouth where I have said the wrong thing in the wrong way at the wrong time in the wrong place. I seem to be more "in-season, on-target in the sweet spot of my day." Things either go better or I respond better, even as difficulties arise because I have trained my ear to hear.

There is a reason for us to spend so much time on this issue. Spiritual intimacy, where we practice the ability to center ourselves on what God may be saying to us in our inner person, enables us to be sensitive to his voice in the midst of hearing so many other voices throughout the day. The question arising as you read this is a legitimate one: "Are you saying that you hear from God?" I am saying everyone hears from God every day. It is just that we do not give him credit. We think it is our creative thought or we think it is some other great idea, but many times, just by an impulse or an urge, he is actually getting through to us.[21]

The second spoke is <u>creativity</u> which we are defining in our context as the ability to have insight on-site, to have a solution or a perspective that may be an alternative to opinions not being presented at the table. Creativity is a

---

[21]See this dramatically explained in the early work of Loren Cunningham, *Is That You God?:Hearing the Voice of God* (Y.W.A.M. Publishing, 2002).

critical piece; the ability to approach things from other angles, and the openness to avoid the circular groupthink in a management system or in a worker's discussion. There is always another way to approach a challenge or an opportunity and creativity is giving permission to us to do it.[22] Simply asking some powerful questions, such as: "If you were able to ask anybody for their opinion who is not in this room, who would you want to ask to see how they would approach this situation?" You may call to mind one of your mentors, a historical person, or an author that you have read. There may be creative solutions that come when we actively listen for the ideas coming from a trained ear that hears God's voice, sometimes opening up a way where there seems to be none.

The third spoke is called perspective and "perspective power" is being able to reframe the context of what we are facing. Many times when we look at a situation we may have one or two or three options and they all seem to be negative or losing, but through coaching or an "honoring conversation," we can go to a place of looking at what would it be like from other perspectives not seen initially until we look for them. By aligning ourselves, quieting ourselves down, and stepping out of the box in our approach, we can come up with four, five, six, or seven different options that were not there initially. Perspective power many times becomes the breakthrough idea that enables a way through where there seems to be none.[23]

---

[22]Robinson, *The Element*, 70ff, notes that the main reason people do not think they are creative is because they have not found their medium in which to express it..

[23]For training on this from an on-line approach, see www.lifeformingcoach.com for the description of Real Talk Training

I can recall situations where it seemed like everyone had exhausted all options until we facilitated people to get in touch with their sense of connection with God, their adjustment to the alignment that he brings, and disengaging from the situation to come back at it later.

Many times they returned with a fresh approach; one that did not seem like it was there before, and it made all the difference.[24]

The second area on our rim is called <u>personal</u> and in the personal quadrant we are focusing on keys that apply personally but can also apply to other areas. The first one is <u>balance</u>. Balance is how we express ourselves in terms of holistic health. In other words, are we a person who is able to give proper balance to the physical, the emotional, the spiritual, and the relational while not overemphasizing any one area to where we are burned out or we lose our margins? Our sense of well-being and balance is projected at work as a person who is able to be steady, reliable, and could be counted on under difficult circumstances to show up and to give our best.

The second area is <u>boldness,</u> which is a spiritual intelligence because it is an inner strength or conviction that allows us to be who we are even under circumstances where we may be tempted to be somebody else, or to fit in to please someone to avoid conflict or a difference of opinion. To have convictions in the market place, and to be bold enough to live them out, is right in line with what people are looking for in co-workers today, more than ever. In too many of the

---

by the author.

[24]This is discussed in more detail in the chapter on the wellness wheel.

practices in the business realm and other key professions, people have been willing to sacrifice principle for their own promotion, but people who live out their convictions and live true to themselves are at peace with themselves. They are bold enough to have the convictions and bold enough to not leave them at the door when they go into their vocation or profession.

The third spoke is <u>integrity</u>, which in many ways can be defined as who we really are under pressure. Integrity is opposite of fragmentation and is meant to be an integration of ourselves both on the job and off the job, meaning that we are not two different people. We can live an integrated life, not segregated. We live a whole life not fragmented.

There is "Madoff madness" in the land today, referring to the perpetrator of a Ponzi scheme that devastated so many innocent people and organizations. It enables principled people to hang up their integrity at the doorpost of financial prosperity. None of us are immune to it and consistent integrity will require a level of transparency that must be in the system and become the norm. A culture of honor at work will allow a new level of checks and balances that must become the norm or we will lose the inheritance we have to give to our children in America.

When we look at our personal life, seeking balance, boldness, and integrity, what we are really building towards is that fourth spoke called <u>alignment.</u> Alignment can be defined as living out our core values and principled ethics.[25] A life

---

[25]See *A Coach Approach to Distilling Personal Core Values* by master coach Diana Gonzalez, available as part of the on-line training mentioned in previous footnotes.

worth living is the same one that we are living out in our homes and jobs.

There is a premium for people who do not put on a spin, a face, or just a presentation. The workplace culture is yearning for people that are authentic, people that are the real deal. In other words, you can count on what they say because whenever they are saying something, it is who they are. They are saying it because they will say it in one place and they will say it in another. You can depend on them. They are living in alignment of their life.

There is nothing pleasant about being out of alignment when you have to have an adjustment for your back or your neck, and nothing as satisfying as the integration of being in alignment and being able to have been adjusted again. As we look at these spiritual quotients we are looking at adjusting ourselves by paying attention to some areas that perhaps have been left at the door of the office or the church, when the whole goal is a life that is integrated.

The third quadrant for a healthy SQ is the <u>family</u> with some of these spokes applying to other areas on intelligence as well. The first foundational to all is a sense of <u>love.</u> This is our ability to live in a judgment-free zone of unconditional love to our spouse and children. This ability to give and receive love enables us to consistently choose to see them above their shortcomings or what they have to measure up to. Instead, we see their potential, where they could be in an atmosphere where they are really believed in, when they have someone else who has faith in them.

Extreme Home Makeover is one of the most gripping reality shows on television today. Each episode presents a compelling story of the power of love in action from a community, a family, and companies who seem to receive as much and more as they give to others. It offers a graphic picture in our culture today of the restoration of more than just a physical building, but the role of the restored home and family as a foundation to all of our spiritual vitality.

The second spoke is <u>servanthood,</u> which is honoring and edifying others in acts of kindness. Choosing to serve their purposes or dreams is giving honor. Sometimes going out of our way to make sure that they have what they need to develop themselves is akin to letting them stand on our shoulders and go beyond where we could have gone in life on our own. Serving our family is one of the greatest ways to create a "culture of honor"[26] in the home and to create young men and women who want less to be served but who thrive in offering service on the job, in the country, and to the nations.

A repeat appearance on our wheel is the spoke of <u>balance</u>. We defined it here as that holistically healthy ability to disengage from work and engage in things that will create family memories, and create family health. Success is to have our children say to us that some of the best memories they have had were in the family times together, both when we did special things, but also when we just ate together and had what I call powerful conversations at the dinner table. I am convinced, as some psychologists have said, that if American

---

[26]"Culture of honor" is a term used by the author that refers to a "creation approach" to another; ie each person has a unique design (personality, fingerprint, DNA), unique desires (core values and passions), unique dreams (lifelong "convergence" moments), and unique destiny (legacy and life purpose). Psalms 139:14-16. By celebrating, rather than tolerating this uniqueness, we honor them and create a communication breeding authenticity, and trust in the home and workplace.

families simply eat together four times a week, we could change the nation.[27] So many families may be in the same room, but they are not really together. We have television, cellphone, or something else is always going on, but if we could recover the art of table talk, of creative conversation, we would recover the art of balance.

Renowned violinist Isaac Rabin used to say that his father would always ask him when he came home, "Did you ask any good questions today?"[28] To be able to have an atmosphere where you could converse and you could enjoy some of the meals together could be one of the greatest places of education for the next generation. I call it transformational table talk at mealtime and tuck-in talk at bedtime, when we simply get some of the greatest conversations and teachable moments talk, and when we experience the joys and sorrows of life together.

This ability to express our lives at home is summed up in the last spoke we are naming, <u>presence</u>. Presence means being fully engaged with our family when we are with them so that when we are eating together we are together. When we are having those special moments we are there 100 percent, being fully present, fully engaged, fully focused on those lives in which we only have such a small part of our day to be together.

The amazing episodes of the Discovery Channel's *Dog Whisperer* are powerful stories of how one man that is "fully present" to the canine kingdom can make such quick and

---

[27]Unpublished interview with Dr. James Dobson of *Focus* on the family and other psychologists.

[28]Unpublished comments from Benjamin Zander, conductor of the Boston Philharmonic, at the International Coach Federation Conference in 2004.

lasting behavioral changes where their owners have failed. Effective coaches call this "being in the moment" and it is a key function of a highly spiritually intelligent man or woman at home and at work.

When you look at SQ in terms of a healthy foundation with God, personal, and our family, then our spiritual life can be meaningfully expressed to our co-workers. In the spokes for the co-workers there is really nothing new here. We have already identified the categories that can apply both at home and at work. Yet out of that ability to nurture, to strengthen, to have something to offer and something to give in the SQ with God, personal, and home, we now can express these on the job, even though it may be a different expression than it is in the family. It is a love that chooses to come out of the self-deception of putting people in a box, or simply not judging them.[29]

Intelligence here is an ability to see people the way you would want them to see you. It means to even choose the best in what we believe about people or how we see them, even when they are not choosing that for themselves. That is love. Anybody can see the weaknesses. It takes a spiritual person to see the solutions or the way through to the strengths. When we get out of that judgment zone into the accepting and believing zone, we will be able to call forth out of people's lives in ways that they would be their best. People will want to work with that kind of co-worker.

Servanthood is choosing to put that love into concrete actions, steps, and behavior in ways that defy one's role or

---

[29]See the powerfully presented explanation of this in The Arbinger Institute's *Leadership and Self-Deception: Getting Out of the Box* (San Francisco: Berrett-Koehler, 2009).

position. I remember a particular job in which I was working on a construction team in a naval base with a coarse group of co-workers. I began practicing the ability to see them and to respond to them in ways that was a little bit extraordinary for them. Without my knowledge some began to look forward to having conversations with me and became transformed by those times we had on the job. Several key leaders today said that those relationships of twenty years ago on the job for those few months became the turning point in their lives. When I reflected on it I realized that this had happened to me as well with people that I worked with and people that had a great impact in my life on the job. They had called me to a higher place of balance, a higher place of alignment. It was servanthood on the job.

Being able to create a culture of honor at work is a mark of SQ. It is accomplished more by affirming and celebrating rather than just tolerating people. This can only consistently happen by <u>alignment</u> of our lives both off and on the job. Living out of our core values means we are making choices that are aligned with those values. It also means, in the integrity spoke, that we are <u>integrated</u>. This is the ability to be an integrated person, whether we are under pressure or whether we are not. It is what people can count on us as delivering when we are enjoying a healthy SQ. A <u>balanced</u> person is one who is fully <u>present</u> to the people on the workplace, fully aware and able to communicate that presence.

When we are ascending a mountain, the dangerous times are when storms may hit us trying to reach the summit, and some of the great stories and heroes that we honor have come out of these storms. These stories are really the stories

48

of spiritual people who were able to live that out under extremely difficult circumstances. Taking that metaphor from the mountain climbers, we believe that the ability to be a spiritual person who is accessible, have a spiritual model that others can feel is attainable, and live a spiritual lifestyle which is relevant to others around us, will be the common practice at healthy workplaces. That is the real deal; not the religious ideal for some, nor is it the religious ordeal that has become the unpleasant reality for others. That is the new deal that people have longed for, and when they see it, when they taste it, and when they touch it, they know that this is the kind of a person that they want to work with. This is the person that they can give their best with.

People really do not leave jobs; they leave relationships. If you and I would aim for excellence in our spiritual quotient, and see ourselves making some progress along this assessment, then we are going to be the type of person that people want to be around. I want to spend my hours on the job with people like this. As we assess ourselves at home and at the workplace, the question of the hour is how can I be on all eight cylinders in terms of my spiritual intelligence and where do I need to be able to shore up in some areas that may be tripping me up and keeping me from being my best. That is the spiritual quotient on the ascent of our mountains.

CHAPTER FOUR
EMOTIONAL INTELLIGENCE

Transformational Intelligences for Home and Work©

Emotional Wheel - EQ

Our second look at intelligences or "intels" that will enable you to create a culture of honor at home and at work is the recently popularized <u>emotional intelligence, EQ</u>. I want to give several research illustrations of this right up front.[30]

"Research in intensive care units has shown that the comforting presence of another person not only lowers the patient's blood pressure, but also slows a secretion of fatty acids that block arteries."[31]

---

[30] This chapter draws largely from the text, *Primal Leadership: Realizing the Power of Emotional Intelligence* by Daniel Goleman, Richard Boyatzis, and Annie McKee (Cambridge: Harvard Business School Publishing, 2002).

[31] Ibid., referencing Lisa Berkman, et al., "Emotional Support and Survival after Myocardial Infarction," *Annals of Internal Medicine* (1992): 6.

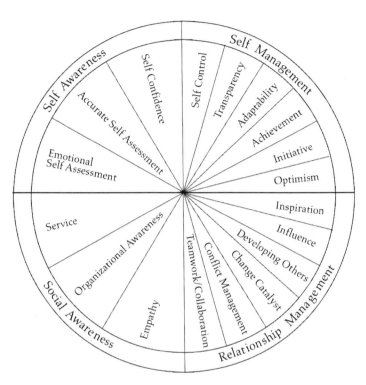

Categories taken from Dr. Daniel Goleman's work on emotional intelligence

More dramatically, where there is incidence of intense stress within a year time period, or other life difficulties, a person who has close relationships that are emotionally healthy is able to be much healthier and effective in their responses. This concept is what researchers have called the ability to mirror or "mirroring."

For example, some studies have demonstrated the effects of conversations where people have started a conversation with their physical bodies, each operating at different rhythms. But by the end of a simple fifteen-minute conversation, the physiological profiles look remarkably similar. Researchers are calling that phenomenon mirroring: the ability to mirror the person who you are with or the ability for them to shape the way you are feeling about certain situations.

When three strangers sit facing each other in silence for a minute or two, the one who is most emotionally expressive transmits his or her mood to the other two without speaking a single word.[32] This same effect holds true in the office, in the boardroom, or on the shop floor. Wherever people are working in groups, they inevitably catch the feelings from another and whether it is jealousy, envy, or euphoria, the discovery of this emotional tone is a critical factor in making a difference in the workplace as a worker, manager, or leader.

People realize intuitively that there is contagiousness from the top. In other words, people take their emotional cues from the top. Even when a boss, manager, or supervisor is not highly visible, the attitude coming from that leader in

---

[32]Daniel Goleman, *Primal Leadership:Learning to Lead with Emotional Intelligence* (Boston: Harvard Business School Press, 2002), 7ff.

terms of the mood of his direct reports, or the domino effect of her emotions, will ripple through the entire organization.[33] The leader's way of seeing things has a special weight. The leaders somehow manage the meaning for a group by offering a way to interpret and to react emotionally in any given situation.

Tremendous research has been coming out on the role of emotional intelligence in the health of an organization, worker, or leadership team. One discovery is a concept called emotional hijacking. For instance, you could look at an international hotel chain to discover what caused the workers to be in bad moods that would communicate negative things to their customers. The most frequent discovery was that the workers who had talked to someone in management and experienced stressful interactions with their bosses led to bad feelings, frustration, disappointment, anger, sadness, disgust, or hurt about nine out of ten times. These interactions were the largest cause of distress more often than customer challenges, work pressure, company policies, or even personal problems.[34] In other words, the relationship with leaders in terms of what they communicated emotionally was the number one factor in the workers' lives in this particular top-of-the-line hotel chain.

---

[33]The leader's emotional impact in work groups: Anthony T. Pescosolido, "Emotional Intensity in Groups" (PhD dissertation, Case Western Reserve University, 2000).

[34]Bosses and bad feelings: John Basch and Cynthia D. Fisher, "Affective Events-Emotions Matrix: A Classification of Job-Related Events and Emotions Experienced in the Workplace," in *Emotions in the Workplace: Research, Theory and Practice,* N. Ashkanasy, W. Zerbe, and C. Hartel, eds. (Westport, CT: Quorum Books, 2000), 36-48.

We recognize the sarcasm when someone will say, "If you are happy just notify your face!" This was a key reason why it was not easy for the McDonald's chain to penetrate Russia when they almost gave up trying to get the post-communism era, depressed generation, front-line server to look a customer in the eye, smile, and ask them how they could help them.

Common wisdom holds that employees who feel upbeat about themselves, about who they are working with, about their job, will likely go the extra mile to please customers and, therefore, improve the bottom line. This has contributed to the awareness of the lifetime value of a satisfied customer. Wal-Mart did a study in which they discovered that the lifetime value of a lost customer was $175,000. That included the money they would have spent as well as the money spent by friends whom they would have influenced in a negative way.[35] So the person who greets you at the entrance of a Wal-Mart is a very important person in terms of creating a climate in the company to enable you to have a good experience!

When we think about what the analysis and research is looking at in terms of the emotional intelligence in the workplace, overall the climate of how people feel about working at a company can account for sometimes 20 percent to 30 percent of business performance. If that is the case, then roughly 50 percent to 70 percent of how employees perceive their organization's climate can be readily traced to the actions of the person that they are directly working under.[36] To be intelligent at work, to be brilliant, requires us to recognize the key role of emotions. This means there is a

---

[35]Unpublished e-mail by Dr. Gary Collins, 2009.
[36]Goleman, *Primal Leadership*, 18.

new kind of leader that is necessary today. A leader who is effective as the world evolves, and who recognizes that leadership is constantly being formed in us and other great leaders, might change their styles, but they do not change their principles. Lasting leaders determine their style by observing and reading their people and seeing what is needed to really resonate or connect with them, including emotionally.

Think through this with me for a minute. Every leadership style is valuable in certain contexts or in certain situations. There is the military commander, top down, no one questions them style. There is only one leader and the rest are followers. The key value here is loyalty and certainly that is what you want when you are in a military situation or when you are in a 911 crisis; you want command and control leadership. Then there is the CEO style, which is the primary business model of communicating vision to others to follow. The quality of the vision is just as important as the quality of the leader. The key value here is productivity, which is the ability to make sure that the company is producing. There is also the entrepreneurial style. These are the pioneers and self-starters. The priority here is being the first to do something and the key value is innovation. All these roles have something to offer. But what we see emerging more and more is that people are really appreciating a leader who also functions in some ways as a coach.

What we mean by a coach is someone who is interested in developing people, not just programs a coach who is making relationships a priority, especially the resonance with people in those relationships, and making teamwork participation as the primary method, rather than simply leadership by command or by memos. The key value being expressed here

56

is the ability to connect to people, and the ability to develop and grow people, as well as make a product or make a profit.

What are the characteristics of a leader, manager, or worker who has some of these coaching values? First of all, they are more highly relational☐ meaning they are more in touch with the tone of relationships and the value of how people are doing relationally. Secondly, they are more emotionally secure so that they are not blown by every wind of emotion that is happening around them, but they are secure in themselves and they empower others through that security. They give people a sense of stepping up to the plate and being who they are meant to be. They listen and they question more than simply telling and commanding. In some ways, they are less formal in structures because there is a more informal characteristic to them. In other words, they find ways to serve others more than being served, that motivates others to want to be the best and to do their best.

When you summarize these different styles, they are all valuable and they are all necessary at certain times. Yet, in some key ways, those who are emotionally intelligent are able to operate in a way that seems to fit the need today more than any other. In other words, when you think about what styles you have seen as a follower and what style you practice most naturally as a leader, the key question is, where could the coaching style help you in your organization? The coaching style takes seriously the emotional health, emotional intelligence, and emotional tone or climate of an organization.[37]

---

[37]See www.lifeformingcoach.com for on-line training, Real Talk Training, that presents these concepts in detail.

We want to unpack the emotional quotient wheel now that we have demonstrated the difference it is making in our vocations. Because of our lengthy introduction, and the extensive writing already on this subject, we will treat the descriptions on this wheel in more brevity than the other wheels. This wheel has spokes in which we can assess our present level of satisfaction and they fall into four categories on the rim. Dr. Daniel Goleman provides both these categories and characteristics in his prolific writings on emotional intelligence. The emotional quotient or the emotional intelligence has been described as <u>self-awareness</u>, <u>self-management</u>, <u>social awareness</u>, and <u>relationship management</u>. The spokes represent aspects that are given in each of these categories.[38]

<u>Self-awareness</u> means, first of all, to be <u>emotionally authentic</u>. It is foundational to discover what it means to be real, authentic, and a person that others can relate to. Authenticity has taken on a higher value in our culture today. It is a gut sense of recognizing what is going on in ourselves, what is going on in others, what is going on in our group, so that we are able to guide some of our decisions based on taking this data into account. Being emotionally authentic is being able to feel, process, own, and discuss those feelings⬜ a key indicator of self-awareness. We recognize that we progress from being unconsciously incompetent to the next stage of being conscious of our incompetence. For us to simply realize, to make ourselves aware, assess ourselves,

---

[38]For definitions of these categories that this author has both built upon and expanded, see Goleman, *Primal Leadership*, 39 and 253-57.

prepare ourselves to be more in tune and in touch with what is going on in and around us, is a great sense of progress.

Self-awareness also involves an accurate self-assessment where we know our strengths and we know our constraints. It is important to realize that we all have them, and as we emphasize our strengths and manage our constraints, we are able to be not only self-aware but also we are self-managed. In today's proliferation of strengths assessments we cannot ignore how key constraints can minimize those strengths and sabotage our ability to express them consistently.[39]

Next is self-confidence, a confidence in the ability to live with our constraints, while knowing that we have self-worth and capabilities despite those constraints. This includes the ability to recognize that others can see our constraints without intimidating us. Many times this is done with a 360 assessment, where others take the same assessment we have done on ourselves, seeing things in us that we do not see ourselves. This is sometimes called blind spots or the Johari Window effect.[40] It is our openness to recognize that others see things in us that we have been blind to, yet still be confident in spite of knowing that everyone else is in the same boat.

Knowing this, all of us can contribute to a climate or a culture of honor at work where we can help each other, cover for each other, and, as a team, strengthen each other.

---

[39]See Flip Flippen and Chris White, *The Flip Side: Break Free of the Behaviors That Hold You Back* (New York: Springboard Press, 2007).

[40]See Alex Lowy and Phil Hood, *The Power of the 2 x 2 Matrix* (San Francisco: Jossey-Bass, 2004).

The next area on the rim of the EQ wheel is <u>self-management</u>. Once we are aware of our unique propensities, then we are able to manage ourselves in spite of them so that we do not have to be dictated by them. The ability for us to make choices that can be the best thing for the group, the company, the situation is to manage our propensity for us to simply "go there on autopilot" all the time. This is the first spoke in this section that Goleman calls <u>self-control</u>.

This ability to understand our emotions, and to make decisions outside of those, is a great sense of development and growth. There is an ongoing inner conversation that happens in an emotionally intelligent person that frees us from only being the prisoner of our patterns or the prisoner of our feelings. We take control. Because emotions are so contagious, especially from leaders to others in the group, "The first task for an intelligent leader is the emotional equivalent of practicing good hygiene."[41] In other words, getting a handle on our own emotions and controlling our lives in spite of them.

Leaders cannot effectively manage emotions in anyone else without first managing their own. To be self-managed really is to be <u>transparent</u>. That is the second spoke under the self-management category. Transparency is not just a virtue for a person, but transparency is an organizational strength. To be transparent at work is about the way we are dealing with people, the way we deal with policies, the way we deal with finances. That authentic openness to others about feelings, beliefs, and actions, allows integrity or the sense of trust in the company or in the leaders. This is a critical factor---the trust factor☐ in terms of what takes place on the job.

---

[41]Goleman, *Primal Leadership*, 46.

Adaptability spoke is about the flexibility in being able to adapt to changing situations or specific obstacles that we may be facing. That flexibility or adaptability is connected to what we may be feeling in the organizational or relational climate or currents. We are managing turning the rudder for the sake of the context or the team or the company.

Achievement spoke is the drive to improve performance, to meet inner standards of excellence. This is another self-managed process with the ability to make the adjustments to achieve something larger then ourselves, even though we may be locked into certain feelings or constraints. It is evidenced in an ongoing effort for lifelong learning and development. Managing our constraints and even our emotions, so we can achieve an excellence with others that we would not normally attempt on our own, is the EQ brilliance at work aspect shown here.

Initiative spoke is being able to be ready to act and seize opportunities. It comes from being prepared, from having clarified our dreams and destiny goals, and then seeing and seizing the moments that contribute to them, such as service, stretching projects, and promotions. It also comes from the discipline of saying "no" to the busy in order to say "yes" to the calling or largeness of our careers and vocational impact.

Finally, under self-management, is the spoke called optimism. This is to intentionally view the upside in any event before taking the downside seriously. Being willing to choose that first, even though you may be wired to see the downside dangers, or feel it is your life calling to point it out, is the self-management of optimism. The ability to manage the propensity towards fear and negativity in the workplace, in a group, or team context, is critical. Optimism is also affirming a creative brainstorm or innovation so that people are validated in their creative perspectives and opinions.

Self-awareness and self-management should be applied first of all in the home. The ability to positively influence the emotional climate of the home is the key for doing so in the office. If there is anything that we have learned over the years in the people-helping professions, it is how dysfunctional leaders and workers many times carry into the workplace the emotional dysfunctions that they have grown up with in the home, seeing what is modeled before them and learning how to live in an environment of emotional dysfunctionality. All of us have baggage so to speak; no one comes from a perfect situation. But to be able to live out this emotional awareness, the ability to accurately self-assess, and then the willingness to be self-controlled, be transparent, be adaptable, take the initiative, and be optimistic at home will enable us to be strong in the workplace. We will be the kind of influencer that is able to be in season, making a difference when it is needed, and being able to influence others at a critical time in the life of a company.

Self-awareness and self-management are the foundation for EQ and once we get this right, the other two will begin to fall into place. The third is <u>social awareness</u> which begins first with the ability to express <u>empathy</u> to others. Simply stated, it is when we are sensing another's perspective and we are taking an interest in their concerns. I think the biggest way this happens for us in terms of emotional intelligence is to hold back from categorizing people or labeling people too quickly. In other words, rather than quickly put a person's position, perspective, or opinion in a category or box, we are willing to take the time necessary to curiously discover the unique perspective that this person has to offer.[42] Then, we can explore it with them, long enough for them to know that we have taken them seriously; they are not just a category but actually have a name with a unique contribution that needs to be heard. The resulting feeling that they have been valued in their perspective is a huge deposit; in a sense it puts a relational equity in the bank account of another person that can be drawn upon when needed in times of change, conflict, or challenges.

Secondly is <u>organizational awareness</u> that enables us to read what is going on in the politics of the company, the relational currents that may be shifting, and the policy tides that may be coming in or going out, or just the tone, resonance, or the emotion of the group of people at work. We know they are all individuals, but there is a collectiveness that is bigger than any individual, even bigger than the sum of the individual. To be aware personally, relationally, and socially, is to read the currents, the winds, and the temperature of what is happening in the organization.

Thirdly is <u>service</u>, which is recognizing and serving those in and through the company and being seen not as one who wants to be served, but as one who wants to serve others. The most important way for this to happen is to be available to the service needs when they are needed and that requires an intentional planning to be present to people through the week. Sometimes simply walking slowly through the hallways can do more for serving than the weekly discussion around the board table.

So we have seen then the social awareness and self-awareness are overlapping quadrants. One can be applied

---

[42] Arbinger Institute, *Leadership and Self-Deception,* 55 ff.

personally and one can be applied for family, as well as in the workplace. Then self-management and relationship management are also quadrants with differing targets. Both of these are connected. Let's target the last quadrant that is the cumulative result of EQ in the first three.

Relationship management begins with the ability to inspire others, to live a life that causes others to want to live bigger, want to live larger, and to want to live better. Many times it is people seeing that despite what might be going on in our personal life, or in the life of the industry or company we are working with, we have an attitude or an ability to shape how others are interpreting the circumstances beyond their control. What inspires them is the way we deal with suffering, the way we deal even with blessing, which contributes to inspire others to live a life that counts, a life that is worthy.

My son is facing his ninth back surgery and has suffered chronic pain for the last fourteen years at a very high level. Even though he is disabled and cannot work for lengthy time frames, he has continued to inspire others to live larger because of how he deals with the circumstances beyond the control of his life.

The second word is influence. Influence is the ability to persuade others, the ability to move others that seem to be stuck, even at times when they do not want to be moved. In patterns of thinking, feeling, or behaving, the ability to influence is really the ability to manage our relationships as workers, leaders, managers, or supervisors in ways that cause people to be willing to continually give us the benefit of the doubts they have about change. To lean on our hope, or on our faith or enthusiasm, is to borrow from us when they do not have it for themselves. Leadership by influence is a leader that is self-aware, self-managed, and then is able to express that relationally to others.

The third word is <u>developing others</u>. This is a main focus of a coach approach to others in which success is measured as much by personal development as in corporate advancement.[43]

Though the two may seem to have different starting points, they both can converge through the skilled leadership of a manager who treats them as equal.

The fourth word is <u>change catalyst</u>. As you assess yourselves in these areas, where have you seen yourself needing to develop the ability to influence the mood or tone of the way people work together? The change catalyst for relationship management is a critical piece, and the ability to initiate, manage, and lead in a new direction comes out of the reservoir of persons who resonate. The word "resonate" is a word in which something about a self-managed and self-aware person causes others to resonate with them, and this resonance, not dissidence, enables a person to change, to influence, to develop, and to inspire others.

That is especially true during times of <u>conflict management</u>, the fifth word in this category. I have verified the truth of this statement: "On the other side of conflicts, courageously faced, you can expect to see an increase, an outcome of growth." We can expect to see "favor from others" because "conflict and the time necessary to deal with it, should never be considered a distraction." Some of the greatest breakthroughs of value clarification and agreements

---

[43]See Joseph Umidi, *Transformational Coaching: Bridge Building that Impacts, Connects, and Advances the Ministry and the Marketplace* (Xulon Press, 2005), 54-62

come only through the doorway of conflict. Firstly, they come when conflict is managed or stewarded by leaders who know how not to avoid destroying relationships in the conflict process, but how to honor, create boundaries, and give "permission" to be in healthy conflict. Secondly, they also come from giving "protection:" to be able to offer healthy ways to deal with conflict by protecting anyone from being disrespected by the communication process in the conflict intervention process itself. Thirdly, it also comes from giving "potency:" the ability to serve those who cannot express themselves clearly under stress or tension by enabling their voice to be heard, not necessarily by being their advocate, but making sure that they feel like equal players on the table when they are in conflict.

All these are tendencies then that create <u>teamwork and collaboration,</u> the last word under this section. The collegial ability to cooperate and to build teams is at the top of the list for workers and managers in this information age. Functional, unlike dysfunctional, teams are the teams that enjoy each other, enjoy the problem-solving process together, and are willing to defer some of their own interests for the sake of others.[44]

Self-awareness, self-management, social awareness, and relationship management all come from the ability to manage families and ourselves first. This foundational awareness will enable us to have the creditability, the confidence, and the fruitfulness of managing others in relationships, in teams, and in the company cultures that we serve. We are saying that emotional intelligence is real. It is as real as IQ. Most people

---

[44]See Patrick Lencioni, *The Five Dysfunctions of a Team: A Leadership Fable.*(San Francisco: Jossey-Bass, 2002).

who are smart intellectually work under leaders that have a lower IQ. What they do have is a higher EQ. A lot of leaders are promoted because their emotional intelligence or emotional quotient is high. Out of that strength and ability, they have credibility for others to willingly follow with enthusiasm. How we assess ourselves on this wheel and then how we consider being coached in areas where we can make adjustments is what this chapter is all about. We can see progress with action steps, smart goals, and specific growth plans for us. This is the mark of a brilliant person, a person who is willing to recognize there is spiritual intelligence and emotional intelligence, and both of these together can make for a healthy home and a happy workplace. Go ahead, "taste and see" how healthy and how happy you can be as you assess and progress in the EQ as part of your portfolio where you live and work.

CHAPTER FIVE
WELLNESS INTELLIGENCE

Transformational Intelligences for Home and Work©

WELLNESS (Physical) INTELLIGENCE -WQ

Welcome to the discussion of the whole aspect of physical intelligence, or as some people better describe it, wellness intelligence. Wellness intelligence is a powerful word combination and it is hard to define. As we reflect on the following, I am sure it will be an "intel" that we will want to move towards throughout our lives.

WQ is not just the absence of a sickness, dysfunction, or of something that is not working. It is the presence of certain things that enable us to be well rounded, and enjoy a well-being. We need to challenge ourselves because, in a sense, everyone has a view of wellness that settles for comparing ourselves to others, rather than in viewing ourselves in terms of our potential.

Joseph L. Umidi

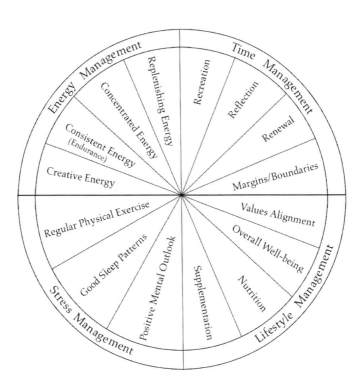

Wellness can include lots of things. Certainly it deals with the mental and physical parts: weight, shape, libido, eating, and sleeping. There are lots of valid ways to discuss and look at it. What we are discovering more than ever today is that many of us have settled for far less in terms of what we can be at any stage of our lives. We drifted into a "growing old" mindset that has kept us working a certain way or in a certain job as if that is all we can muster. A lot of us have become far less than we could be, and, as a result, America is not very intelligent compared to other developed nations when it comes to our lifestyles, stress levels, obesity, and to some of the diseases to which we have succumbed. If we were to evaluate wellness just in terms of the amount of chemicals and pills that we are inundated with, we are not doing very well in terms of the rest of the world.

Whether you are an expert in nutrition, a physician, or someone who is attempting to just feel better about what you do, we need to recognize that wellness encompasses a lot of interconnected and important parts of our lives, like our emotions and our creativity. Some of the very things we have already mentioned in SQ and EQ are encompassed in defining wellness, and in many ways are affected by the way we look at wellness.

There are two things the World Health Organization has said recently that I agree with. Two obstacles to a vibrant health and longevity are ignorance and complacency.[45] Yet, there is more information available today on how to have a healthy lifestyle at home and at work, and how to have a

---

[45]More information on this is available from nutritional coaches Dr. Jerry and Sharon Graham. See www.thecoachingpair.com.

healthy workplace environment. The challenge is not a shortage of information, but in sifting facts from fallacy.

A lot of people are confused; they do not know what to believe and how to move forward. Some of us have enough information, but do not have the motivation to do anything with it. For instance, just about everybody I talk to has heard somewhere along the line how artificial sweeteners are not good for them, but many drink continually five or six diet drinks a week, or even worse, some drink those in a daily basis. Education itself is not the answer. People have to realize the value of wellness, of being physically intelligent, and the difference it can make in their lives.

Certain insurance companies know that value, as well as governments who are paying for school systems and for health insurance. People who deal with the cost in our culture of healthcare know the difference that wellness can make. They recognize it as a crisis in our nation, especially in terms of our gross national product. Bottom line, wellness intelligence is really a personal responsibility.

The ability for us to read our own personal signals regarding our own wellness is to be in touch with both our emotions and what our body is saying to us about itself, and to align ourselves with who we are authentically. We can be fit in terms of the gym definition, but the way we eat can really be signs of a lack of wellness. In a sense, health is the state in which all of the systems of the body are working optimally so that even though you may look like you are in shape, the core questions center around the quality of all the systems: the immune systems, the nutrient systems, etc. In essence all the wellness systems are functioning properly.

I remember, for instance, when I was "lean and mean as a high school and college wrestling machine." Sure, I could get my weight down, but then as soon as I qualified in the weigh-in for my class, I would stuff myself with cupcakes, pizza, or Big Mac's and I would literally gorge myself with unhealthy foods. My lifestyle of eating was anything but well in terms of what I was doing to myself. So, looking fit and being well are not the same, unless we apply a proper understanding of wellness that includes the ability to manage our life in some key areas.

What are those areas? On our wellness intelligence assessment wheel, we have the opportunity to actually measure our present level of competence or balance in any of the areas divided up on the edge of the perimeter in four categories: energy management, time management, stress management, and lifestyle alignment.

Let us first talk about time management.

We have all heard and experienced the "tyranny of the urgent."[46] These are the things screaming at us all the time to be done and should have been done yesterday, and they keep us from doing what is really important. We understand we can be busy all day, busy about trivial things or only urgent things, but never busy about the things that can bring a sense of wellness to us. What are those things that would bring wellness in terms of our time?

Time management really begins with the role of recreation before considering the demands of vocation. Some of you are thinking, "I thought time management began with ordering

---

[46]See Richard Swenson, *The Overload Syndrome* (Colorado Springs: NavPress Publishing Group, 2004). See also, Richard Swenson, *Margin: Restoring Emotional, Physical, Financial, and Time Reserves to Overloaded Lives* (Colorado Springs: NavPress Publishing Group, 2004)   for great help in this area.

my workday?" Time management begins with ordering our rest day. When we understand the creation accounts in the book of Genesis, we see man was not created on the last day of the week so that he could rest from work. Man was created on the first day of rest in order for him to be prepared to manage the rest of his workweek in life.[47] When we recognize that recreation in many ways is re-creation, we are ready to approach time management properly. In other words, it is the ability for us to re-create ourselves physically, emotionally, spiritually, and be strengthened and prepared for what may lie ahead that makes time management effective in our work life.

There are many accounts about the great breakthroughs in science of people working long and hard. They would stay at the laboratory with their microscopes for hours on end. But many times, as hard as they worked, it was not until they recreated that they re-created. It was not until they got on the tennis court or in the swimming pool or in the shower that they got the key breakthrough: an idea, the formula, and the thing that was eluding them when they were perspiring at the worktable.

WQ in time management is living out the reality that consistent creativity does not come from tired people. You may hit a home run every now and then, but consistently being able to think, work, and innovate only comes when there is a pattern of recreation. Recreation or re-creation is not optional. We have to disengage ourselves, unplug ourselves from the matrix, to be able to do things that are not normally what we do by reading e-mail or listening on a cell phone or text messaging. It is to do some things, or nothing at all, that creates in us another ability to approach the

---

[47] Read Gen., chapter 1, and note the numbering of the days.

workplace from a different point of view. Time management then begins with making sure that we build into our schedules recreation time.[48]

Part of the challenge I find with people today is that we have lost the art of <u>reflection</u>. This is the second aspect of time management. It is not just to rearrange our lives to get more done in the week, but to make sure that we build into our lives the ability to reflect over some of the experiences we are having throughout the day or the week. I could have forty years' experience in some area, but in many ways it may be just one-year experience and repeated thirty-nine times. What I mean by that is <u>experience does not teach us anything</u>; it is the <u>reflection and feedback on the experience which</u> enables us to <u>glean, draw, learn, and accelerate our develop</u>ment from it.

Think about the amount of time people on the job go to workshops, in which they may have to cram two days of work in one day, and then when they come back they have to catch up to all the e-mails and all the things that have become urgent. After a week or two, they have forgotten what the workshop was about or what they determined to do with the workshop training. Unless we build in to any kind of learning experience the ability to reflect, to lock in the learning, and to reorder our lives by it, we will not have the sustainable change in development and the accelerated growth that we are

---

[48]In training sessions around the world we consistently find that people have not reflected on the importance of recreation and have little room for play, hobbies, or re-creative rest in their lives. Simply seeing its critical role to creativity has unleashed hundreds of e-mails of gratitude for what it has meant to their personal, family, and work lives.

looking for and need in the workplace. Without this basic WQ, we will not be well enough to have learned from the experience but will simply have to go around and around that learning mountain again.[49]

Time management also requires us not only to build in recreation time and reflection moments after action events or intense experiences, but also to have time for renewal. Robert Clinton's research on people and leaders that finish well revealed a key factor: they have repeated times of intentional renewal in their lives.[50] That means they have learned to take a Sabbath or a day off, and have learned to shut down, disengage, and do a sabbatical.

A sabbatical may be a term that is not used in the marketplaces; perhaps it is more of an academic and a religious term. It simply means we have an intentional plan or a process not only to disconnect us from something, but also connect us to those things which bring physical, emotional, mental, and spiritual renewal.[51] The ability to intentionally plan what renews, revives, and refreshes us is one of the

---

[49]Ongoing research on the ROI of adding coaching on the back end of corporate workshops shows a strong trend for sustainable change and results than simply having workshops alone.

[50]See Robert Clinton, *The Making of a Leader: Recognizing the Lessons and Stages of Leadership Development* (Colorado Springs: NavPress Publishing Group, 1988).

[51]The Bible refers to a sabbatical year, which is every seventh year, during which the land, according to the law of Moses, had to remain uncultivated (Lev. 25:2-7; Exod. 23:10, 11, 12; Lev. 26:34, 35). Some companies offer unpaid sabbatical for people wanting to take career breaks with policies and guidelines readily available. This is a growing trend in the United Kingdom, with 20 percent of companies having a career break policy.

greatest benefits of WQ, whether it is music, intense times in the outdoors, or times with family. Those are critical for us to finish well, not just get to the finish line or white knuckling ourselves up the mountain, but the ability to finish strong, to still have our breath, to be able to enjoy the view at the top.

That is the difference for a person who has wellness intelligence, who is able to manage their time, recreation, reflection, and renewal, and then establish margins and boundaries to make sure it happens when it is supposed to. Any leader will tell you that if you do not put in your calendar the things that are important to you, you do not make boundaries around them; your calendar will be filled by someone else's agenda, someone else's wellness issues. In other words, you will always be busy. The question is will you be busy about someone else's wellness or will you be busy about the agenda that is well for you.

The only way we will know the answer to that question is to have margins and boundaries. When we live without margins, we live on the edge; there is no room for the breakdown or the flat tire. There is no room for a financial setback since many of us are only three paychecks away from homelessness. We live without margins, without savings accounts, without time margins, and without room for any interruptions or even emergencies. But when we build margins into our lives, it is amazing what that can mean when our lives are suddenly out of order, in disarray, or interrupted. We can still have room to breath, instead of feeling like we are between a rock and a hard place. Effective time management from a wellness intelligent person includes those key spokes in our lives being assessed and managed.

That takes us to an interesting concept called energy management. One of my favorite Bible passages, Psalms 139, says that we are "fearfully and wonderfully made" and even marvelous in God's sight. While we were in our mother's womb God designed and formed us. If you look at the Hebrew words used in the passage, it actually gives a sense in which there is a uniquely designed chromosomal pattern, like our DNA print, but there is also a unique personality, a unique temperament that is being addressed. It is good scholarship to say there is a unique biorhythm or the way we handle our energy flow implied in this creative description.[52]

In any one family you can see one child is mellow and always so quiet, and the other is hyper and going nonstop. There are two uniquely designed, fearfully and wonderfully made children, that are marvelous in God's sight, but they have different ways of dealing with energy. Energy management says it is not just about how you rearrange your time; it is about how you schedule the things in your time that match your energy flow throughout your day.

Energy management means first of all looking at the spoke called <u>creative energy</u>. In other words determining when you are at your best? When do you feel the most creative? Is it late at night, or early in the morning? Is it in a certain time of day or in a certain context? Those are the places, as you understand your uniqueness in your energy patterns, which you would want to be able to apply the most important part of your workday, the most important meetings, the most important conversations, and the most important projects.

---

[52]Psalms 139:13-16 contains thirteen Hebrew words whose meaning corresponds to medical research on cells, chromosomes, and DNA "ladder" as seen in *Strong's Exhaustive Concordance, Hebrew Dictionary of the Bible,* the *World Book Encyclopedia,* and *The Science Library.*

Creative energy management starts with building your work schedule around the ways in which you can be your best at the best moments of your day.

One sense in which we can encourage a "culture of honor" at work is when we honor people's unique design by saying that we want to not just schedule lives around the time clock, but schedule lives around the biological clock, the energy clock. Each of us can learn to adjust our clocks if necessary by not denying or just tolerating that biological reality, but by assessing, learning how to celebrate, and stewarding it. Energy management begins with assessing where you are most creative in your day, and determining at what points and in what ways to apply that creativity to the most important parts of your day.

The second spoke is <u>consistent energy</u>. Because we need various levels of energy throughout the demands of the day we need to have a consistent reserve to be able to focus our energy at the key points, at the key times, or at the key issues of our workday. There is an ability to have an irreducible minimum consistent energy that is always there through the day and the week. This comes from the art of learning how to fuel your machine, the wonderfully made organism that only you know how to best program.

As a professor I know that I would have certain challenges during certain times of the day and of the week. I watch students struggling during the day when their energy levels were dipping and they default to eating chocolates, diet sodas and drinks, caffeinating themselves with the latest energy broth. It certainly could have something to do with how bored they are with my lectures, but the message here is that they are getting a quick hit to stay awake or stay engaged, and then they would come down that slippery slope as fast as they spike up. They are mature adults in many areas but do not have an understanding of WQ. They have not learned how to fuel the machine of their body in such a way they could come to a certain level and just hum at that level throughout the day until they are called on for a particular time to have more energy. When I learned to do that☐ how to eat a certain way for consistent energy☐ I trained to fuel my body with proper proteins and the amount of times I would eat throughout the day. I became sensitive to my body's voice and able to manage my energy, not just my time.

The third spoke on the WQ wheel is <u>concentrated energy</u>. This is the energy that it takes for us to get "in the zone." Those of us who understand athletics, whether it is marathon running or whether it is weight lifting or whatever, know that there is a place where you get to that is unique for focused energy. Often times you first hit the wall, but you just keep on going until you are so focused about what you are doing that it just seems to carry itself. There are issues in the workday and week; some that we know of and can be prepared for, and some that we are not. When called upon for either, we have to be able to step up from the consistent energy platform to a full-out concentrated "in the zone" energy.

We need to learn that energy management enables us to do that as long as we understand the ability to disengage in order to replenish ourselves. When you study the athletes, there is no sport that is twelve months throughout the year and there is no athlete that is going 100 percent all the time.[53] Athletes

---

[53]See Jim Loehr and Tony Schwartz, *The Power of Full Engagement: Managing Energy, Not Time, Is the Key to High*

have learned that after they have given their best at a particular quarter in a game or a particular race around laps, it is time to recover for the next demand of concentrated energy.

That leads to the last area, which is <u>replenishing energy</u>, the art of recovery. That is the genius of wellness intelligence. It is learning what it takes for you and me to recover after a concentrated, intense meeting with someone, teamwork or brainstorming project, or whatever it may be, and to be able to build that in our schedule as an intelligent factor so we do not go from one concentrated expenditure to the next. WQ means we are able to continually have some consistent energy, and then when we have a concentrated energy release, we are able to replenish energy as the art of recovery that takes place for us emotionally, mentally, physically, and spiritually. I have seen too many leaders who have done great programs or building projects, and then on the other side of that they seem to have crashed. They were living on an adrenalin rush for so long and they did not have the intelligence to know how to replenish themselves. They lacked the WQ to have known that the goal was not to achieve their goal; the actual goal of their lives was to be well once that goal was achieved. So wellness management begins with intelligence, time management, and energy management.

The next quadrant on the rim of the WQ wheel is <u>stress management</u>. Stress can be both good and bad for us. When you make a hardened hammerhead, the stress that is put on that hammer enables it to pound a nail. But if there is too much stress applied to the forming of that hammerhead, it

Performance and Personal Renewal (New York: Simon and Schuster, 2004) for a thorough presentation of this phenomena.

can actually cause it to brittle, crack, and crumble. So it is
with stress. Stress can be good for us. It can actually enable us
to be formed in certain ways. But too much stress, especially
without the ability to manage it properly, can actually crumble
us. What is amazing about stress is that many times it is just
our interpretation of it, our mental outlook about it, that
becomes the key to managing it.

The first thing about stress management is the ability to
have a positive mental outlook. We need to be able to
reinterpret the stress of our lives in ways that do not
exacerbate the crumbling effect, but accelerate the hardening
effect. This is the ability to make or form us in the anvil of
our lives to be stronger and be leaned on in time of need by
others. Studies have demonstrated that the chemical reactions
secreted on the anticipation of going to the frontline in a war
zone are the same chemical reactions that are secreted when
you are watching your bride come down the aisle in your own
wedding ceremony. The difference is simply the
interpretation of that stress. It is the same chemical, it is the
same stress issue, but our positive mental outlook at our
wedding day, compared to the day we are thrust into the
frontline in a war zone, are two different interpretations and
two different results.[54]

This ability for us to reinterpret our stress in this way helps
us to reframe it; the ability we noted earlier in emotional and
spiritual intelligence can be done in numerous ways. We can
take if from a God perspective, from a legacy perspective, or

---

[54]In our response to stress the two main systems involved are the
hypothalamic-pituitary-adrenal (HPA) axis and the SNS. These are
activated primarily by an area in the brain stem called the locus
coeruleus; the SNS secretes epinephrine and norepinephrine.

from a generational perspective. The question here to us might be, "If you want to look back at what is happening today when you are ninety-five, what would you want to be said about you and the way you are responding to this stress?" Rather than simply responding from an immediate gratification viewpoint we are being empowered to respond in a way that is writing "my story," "my legacy," and my "generational contribution" in life.

The second key critical to stress management is the ability to have <u>sleep management</u> or <u>good sleep patterns</u>. Sleep is a necessary element to strengthening our bodies and immune systems to deal with stress, and even to have the kind of mental attitude about stress throughout our day that we need. So many people are discovering that they are having sleep apnea[55] problems. They are not able to get a deep sleep in the night. When they make the corrective change in their lives to overcome it, everything about their day, everything about their job, everything about their stress seems to take on a new meaning. Why? Because they've slept well, their patterns of sleep have been altered, and they are strengthened.

Sleep patterns are critical even if it's the pattern to take a quick power nap in the middle of the day. Many stories of people who found that ability to change sleep management discovered that it changes everything. Look at the cultures who understand siestas or who are able to take a break during the day without guilt or shame. So many cultures with many healthy patterns have a wellness intelligence built into the

---

[55]The National Heart Lung and Blood Institute estimates that more than 12 million American adults have obstructive sleep apnea. More than half of the people who have this condition are overweight.

culture regarding the ability to disengage and to have a good sleep situation even at a certain time of day.

Our last emphasis to be able to deal with stress is the role of <u>regular physical exercise</u>. The stress we put on ourselves physically in proper exercise is the key thing that burns off the accumulated stress in our bodies from anxiety, the problems and concerns we take on emotionally, spiritually, and mentally throughout the day. Regular physical exercise is not an option, and the good news is if you've been like many who've only made it an option, one that you've not activated very consistently over your life, you can start at any time and see an immediate result.[56]

It's not too late to begin to slow down the aging process and be able to actually feel so much better through something as simple as stretching.

One study published fifteen years ago by doctors from Tuffs University[57] described what is called the "disability zone." This is defined as the zone that a person can enter where they can't take care of their own daily needs. They need help with their shoes, or help to go to the bathroom, or any kind of assistance. The key discovery with bio-intervention is that simply doing nothing more than incorporating some aerobic and strength building exercise, along with making small changes to your diet, will have an immediate impact. No matter when you perform that bio-intervention, whether you do it at fifty, fifty-eight, or sixty-five years old, it immediately alters the slope of your decline into the disability zone. You can actually see that the

---

[56]Ibid.

[57]Found in the book, *Biomarkers: The Ten Keys to Prolonging Vitality.*

beginning of physical exercise and wellness intelligence at any time causes the slope to change immediately. Instead of hitting the disability zone at sixty, you can hit it at eighty-five, or instead of at eighty-five, you can hit it at one hundred! This is great news and encouragement for us, that there is an immediate value in practicing wellness intelligence which deals with stress through positive mental outlook, good sleep patterns, and regular physical exercise.

This takes us to the final quadrant in this assessment wheel on wellness intelligence: lifestyle management. What's lifestyle management? It is aligning our lives according to how we are fearfully and wonderfully made, focusing not only on our unique design, but also on our unique desires. It means there are certain values and passions that are unique to me: things that I really want to live for, things I would be willing to die for, things I would pound the table for if they are not happening in my life, things I am so excited to see happening in life. Our goal is to have values alignment, which is the first spoke in this last section.

The Oscar winning movie, *Chariots of Fire*, featured the life of Eric Liddell back in the Olympics of the 1930s, who made a decision to follow his passions. When he had to run a race he was not prepared for because he refused to run on Sunday in which his own race was scheduled, his sister argued with him to just leave the Olympics and go on to his chosen calling as a missionary in China. Eric told her that he would go on to China soon, but first he had to run. His famous line to her was, "When I run, I feel God's pleasure."

When there is something that we feel so passionately about that we are willing to align our lives around those desires, we actually are living with WQ. Our face radiates and our lives resonate when we are aligned, as compared to living in conflict or dissonance with our core values and passions. We want to encourage you to find a coach who can help you understand how to know what you value and how to live a life aligned around those values.[58]

The second area is called <u>nutrition</u>, which is all about building a healthy immune system. Recently the FDA revised its food group percentages to keep up-to-date with the latest research on nutrition.[59] The medical profession, by and large, is trained to focus on diagnosing an illness, i.e., labeling it, and then based on that diagnosis, to prescribe a substance to suppress the symptoms. Rarely do they address the behavior that precipitated the illness in the first place. Much of that behavior is connected to the cellular level of activity. Some are now defining health as the condition where our cells are functioning properly. Nutrition awareness, assessment, and management, including adequate hydration and recognizing the key difference between processed and fresh foods, are now a foundation for every young parent who wants to raise healthy children. It is also a key to the favor and promotion in the workplace that has been before us since the ancient story of Daniel in the Bible.

The third area is focused on <u>supplementation</u>. After researching this topic it became clear that it should be a separate category than nutrition, despite the ongoing debate on its value. There's now so much air time devoted to nutrition and supplementation that even the American Medical Association has finally come out in 2009 and said they believe that you need to have supplementation if you are

---

[58]See www.lifeformingcoach.com for help on this topic.
[59]See www.fda.gov for more information.

going to be eating nutritiously.[60] This is not our grandfather's soil conditions; therefore, the quality of the foods that we eat are so much less able to give the full nutrition that we need. The booming supplemental industry has certainly been in conflict with the medical industry for so long but finally has support, at least to find a rational and financially intelligent way to deal with supplements for nutrition. Bottom line, we are not able to get the nutrition we need by normal living; thus, nutrition and supplemental intake are necessary today.

The final area to assess is both a spoke under lifestyle management but also qualifies as the end result of the entire WQ wheel. We are simply calling it overall well-being. After twelve years of training coaches worldwide, we have recognized that alignment of our lives results in immediate and sustainable overall well-being. How well is it with our bodies, with our spirit, with our emotions, with our soul? There's an old classic song, "It is well with my soul," and that wellness is available for each of us when we have our "intels" operating at the highest level.

There is no mysterious disconnect between our body, soul, and spirit. We are all connected, we are integrated. What we do with one affects the other, whether it's an aspect of stress on the job, or stress on the travel to and from the job. There is enough information now on the ecosystem of our lives to increase our wellness intelligence quotient. Yet it is much more than information. The key to transformation is motivation and what we've discovered is that through the role of coaching, we can add the motivation factor that makes the difference.

---

[60]See www.unitedmedicalnetwork.com.

With a peer coach that provides support, encouragement, and accountability, many of us who know better are able to do better. We can tell anybody they have a choice at the table to pick which is better for them□ an apple or a donut. Everyone will mentally pick the apple. Yet it is interesting that almost everyone is going to reach for the donut. What is lacking here is not always the knowledge, but it's the structure and the accountability to implement good choices. That's what coaching brings to the table. When a client works with a coach they work out their goals together. It's something that the client is motivated to achieve and the coach simply provides support, encouragement, and accountability.

I will never forget how many times at the gym that I would get frustrated every January 2 when all of a sudden you couldn't get to the machines. So many people had made a New Year's resolution and purchased an expensive gym pass. Some of them even hired a trainer so they wouldn't get hurt. Yet predictably, just six weeks later, we knew things would be back too normal. Why was that? Because when people hit the wall they forgot to be in touch with the core thing in the first place that motivated them to come to the gym, or maybe the reason for their motivation wasn't big enough or compelling enough to get them through the wall. They lacked the coach. They lacked the reason why they were there. They lacked the support, encouragement, and accountability it would take to achieve it.

As you review your self-assessment on this wellness wheel you can make the choice that will give you sustainable change. Discover where you may be intelligent now in a certain area, but where you need to come up, and perhaps, can't pull yourself up by the bootstraps. That itself is the foundation of all intelligence; and recognizing what is needed is another aspect of encouragement in your life. Perhaps you need a coach? Certainly if you get it right in this area with wellness, if it is well with your soul, well with your mind, well with your emotions, well with your body, you will be the kind of person who's going to be able to climb that mountain, or be able to help others achieve their summits. We all want to achieve sustainable peak performance on the workplace and in the home because well people are well rounded, well integrated both at home and at work. That's the goal of the transformational intelligences: creating a culture of honor at home and work because we have integrated these "intels" in our home and work life together.

CHAPTER SIX
FINANCIAL INTELLIGENCE

Financial Wheel   FQ
Transformational Intelligences for Home and Work©

FINANCIAL INTELLIGENCE FQ

Financial intelligence, or as some people might call it the financial quotient, is foundational because it impacts every other intelligence. No matter how competent we may be in any area as it applies to any vocation or "mountain" that we are targeting in our calling or in our professional career, the role of finances runs like a river through all those mountains. It is the "intel" that can affect all the rest. I have discovered personally that debt reduction or debt elimination is a key to dream realization. Some of the greatest dreams that people have had for their careers or callings have been influenced negatively by the inability to understand some basic principles of financial intelligence.

Joseph L. Umidi

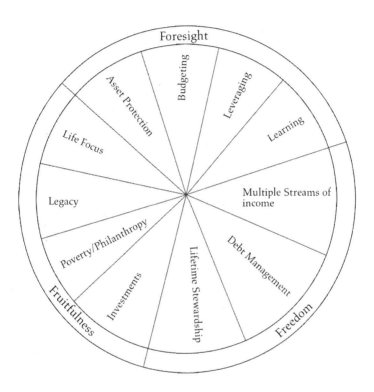

What is financial intelligence? One definition is simply this: realizing that money matters. Financial intelligence is having the right job, the right focus in the job, the right energy for the job, and the right lifestyle off the job. What we are aware of today is that financial intelligence means less financial bondage and more financial freedom in our lives. The other day, I was at a restaurant and I was noticing that the waitresses were over seventy years old. I reflected on how much intelligence did they have in their thinking and planning that at seventy, seventy-five, and eighty they are still out looking for tips in the fast-food restaurants.

Many people pay attention to the things that make them successful in a particular career or mountain but have never paid enough attention to the financial area, so they have financial problems over their lives, unsolved financial issues that carry all through their careers and calling. There is no substitute for having a great financial team around you, including certified financial planners, CPAs, and others. However, the subtle danger here is to let the "experts" handle all of our money matters while we go on with our lives and remain at our present elementary levels of financial knowledge. We cannot abdicate our financial futures to others, but only delegate to them areas of assistance while we grow in the knowledge of solving financial problems and opportunities ourselves.

Money matters, but we need to value money without being valued by it. It means avoiding the culturally acceptable "poverty spirit" that ignores this topic and thinks money is of no value, and carry on with our careers or vocations as if money did not matter. Another wrong attitude is a "prosperity spirit" where somehow we have the sense that money itself or the accumulation of it is the equation of value or of intelligence.

Financial intelligence is realizing money matters and that money matters in the aspect of all the other areas of our significance. Money makes a difference. It makes a difference on how effective we will be on our vocational impact. Recognizing that the issue is our attitudes towards our finances, not our actual financial situation, is important. Our attitudes towards our financial problems may be avoidance or ignorance or fear or frustration, but it is our attitude about our financial problems that creates our financial problems because all of us will discover that we will increase our financial intelligence by the way we deal with our financial challenges.[61]

The reality is that the majority have ongoing financial problems. They never have enough. They use credit to cover their reality of never having enough. They continually find themselves set back by the increased costs of living that they did not take into account. They are paying unnecessary taxes on any increase in their income and do not realize that they could give themselves, on average, a 34 percent raise by eliminating their debt and its resulting interest payments. They find themselves with very few financial margins for emergencies, no financial planning for retirement, and limited financial advice coming from others who are in the same boat as they are.[62]

---

[61]Many of the foundational principles of this chapter are taken from Robert Kiyosaki, *Increase Your Financial IQ* (New York: Business Press, 2008).
[62]Ibid., 3-4.

There is a large group of people who may need something more basic than this chapter's focus, perhaps more like financial literacy. Because of a lack of basic training from the home, school system, and churches, many do not have the foundations that are necessary to survive the information age and its competing and confusing messages on economics. Like the famous opening statement from the champion coach Vince Lombardi to his team returning to training camp each season, "This is a football," Many need to cover the basics before assessing themselves on this wheel. However, those who have read this far are qualified to accelerate their development and intelligence in this critical area.

But the rich also have financial problems and they may need some help in the area of financial intelligence. Some of them have too much money such that they do not know how to steward properly, or they have an increased need to keep their money safe and invested. There are a number of people with money who cannot tell the difference between friends who like them or friends who like them for their money. So those with money need smarter financial advisors. They need more financial education to keep up with the responsibility of having money. Unfortunately, those with money may have a harder time raising grateful, balanced, and hardworking children. Inevitably, they are constantly dealing with excessive government taxes.[63]

The reality is that we need financial intelligence whether we do not have enough or whether we have too much. Financial intelligence is a key aspect of our vocational impact. We used to think that simply hard work, a good education, and a good job is the answer, but that alone will not solve our

---

[63]Ibid.

financial problems. What solves our financial problems is financial intelligence and financial intelligence comes from becoming a financial problem solver. This comes from experience with feedback and feedback with reflection.

What we are discovering is when we have these "intel" wheels and use them as a tool of self-assessment with feedback from others, including coaches who can help us process the data from our assessment and enable us to move forward. Then we are going to get the maximum value from the financial intelligence process, from the wheel of assessment and the ability to move forward.

These are some of the statements we hear from people who are really asking for the intelligence needed to solve those problems: "I have given up on my dreams because I do not have the money or time to pursue them; I do not earn enough to retire; I am running out of money; I do not like my job, but I cannot afford to quit; I am deeply in debt; I have no money for my child's education; I cannot afford that medical work; I cannot see when I am going to be able to buy a home."

Because many of us have missed what I call financial literacy because our homes, schools, and churches have left that out of the equation, the work of financial intelligence seems daunting to us, and we opt to choose simply trying to achieve financial security rather than financial freedom. What I mean by that is our target is just to earn enough to get to retirement. Yet, in many ways, by settling for that status, we can unknowingly trap ourselves as prisoners in our own offices, the Billy Lomans of *Death of a Salesman*, and we do not know that the keys to the prison door is financial intelligence. The key is not more money; the key is more financial intelligence.

By knowing these "intels" we are more likely than 95 percent of our co-workers to have solutions to our financial problems. We divided these financial "intels" into three categories. Along the rim of your wheel are the names of those categories and then there are the spokes coming from each of those categories in which you are to assess yourself from zero to ten in the area of your perceived competence.

The first category is <u>financial freedom</u>. Financial freedom is depicted in this category with the first spoke of <u>multiple streams of income</u>, MSI. That means we need to make more from more sources. It does not mean we need to have to juggle two or three jobs but that we can discover how to have two or three incomes from the skills, intellectual property, or expertise that we have but may not be realizing its value. Every person or family can begin their quest for financial freedom by assessing and exploring the launching and life-long development of these other income streams.

My father was a tremendous worker who built the veterinary division for a major pharmaceutical corporation. When they brought in new management to take over the company they wanted my father to do some rather unethical things that he would not do. He ended up having to leave his career, his mountain, with a $100 a month pension for the rest of his life. He did not leave my mother much, did not leave an inheritance for me, or his children's children.

He was a good man, but he did not have multiple streams of income.

Let's be clear that money does not make you financially intelligent, but the process of making more money does. You can get more money from a lottery or simply a family inheritance, but many of us have personal stories of people we know who are less intelligent after a great windfall of money then they were even before. They spent it poorly and they wound up deeper in debt and many times in a crisis because of it.

Robert Kiyosaki says over and over in his books that true financial intelligence is learning to solve smaller problems in order to qualify to solve bigger problems. So it is more about the joy of learning rather than the fear of failing.

In the first spoke on our wheel of multiple stream of income the first question might be, "How many streams?" Some people say we should have at least five.[64] I do not have a formula for that, but what I am saying is that everyone should consider that they ought to have several income streams to help them stay focused in their ability to live a life on target for their dreams and destiny as an individual or a family.

The second freedom spoke is <u>debt management</u>. Debt management is a major issue today. *Forbes* magazine interviewed the top 400 successful people regarding what they believed was critical to success. It is very interesting that the overwhelming majority of responses came up with the same decision: to be debt free and to stay debt free.[65] Can it get any simpler?

The situation that we find ourselves in today is one that we have not seen in quite a while. Back in the 1920s, 98 percent of the people were mortgage free and if you had a mortgage you were considered odd. Since 1962 98 percent of people

---

[64]See Robert Allen, *Multiple Streams of Income: How Ordinary People Make Extraordinary Money Online* (New Jersey: John Wiley & Sons, 2004) who recommends ten streams.

[65]Slide presentation by Chris Poole on financial freedom seminar, October 2008.

have a mortgage and if you do not have a mortgage it is considered odd.[66] We have moved from a different way of thinking regarding debt.

We live in a society today where we are comfortable being in a culture of debt. We do not care how much debt we have; we just want to know what the monthly payments will be. Many of us use our homes as an ATM machine. Today, the average American carries, just in consumer debt alone, $38,000 not including a mortgage. The average number of credit accounts for each American is twenty-two. Seventy percent of Americans live paycheck to paycheck. Forty percent spend more then they earn each year. Seventy-seven percent have no savings and today is the first time since the Great Depression that we have a negative savings rate in the United States. Seventy-five percent of Americans are three paychecks away from bankruptcy and we are really in one of the most amazing times of economic turmoil that we have seen ourselves in years.[67]

What we are saying is very simple and clear: we need to find the most accelerated way to zero debt that is possible. There are lots of ways available and I recommend you do something other than what you have been doing, if you want to see different results. There are strengths and weaknesses in any system that you choose.

However, the simple method of putting money in envelopes and paying down one card to the next to the next, though it may have worked for our great grandparents, is not the most accelerated way today that is possible, nor desirable

---

[66]Ibid.
[67]Combines statistics from David Ramsey's financial presentation and previous presentations mentioned..

in terms of the situations we face. I am recommending to you what thousands have been using for the past several years from the latest software developments. One product is called the "Money Merge Account," a sophisticated software algorithm program with back-up tech support and education support that is easy to use. It enables you to accumulate quickly a six-month savings account and then to be able to allow your money to be in the right place at the right time and to be able to pay off interest as quickly as possible. Independent researchers have confirmed that it has been the best tool on the market to accelerate debt reduction.[68]

The third spoke under the category of financial freedom is what we are calling lifestyle stewardship, captured in the old hymn, "It's a gift to be simple..." We can choose priorities in our lives and we can choose to live more simply so that we can prioritize our freedom from debt, and then maximize our ability to help others find the same. That is an important principle not everybody agrees with. Some people think you should live above your means or stretch yourself to grow. I believe that choice is yours, but we put the spoke here in the freedom wheel because it is freedom to be able to never use all that you have at your disposal. It is freedom to dial back to live for other priorities. Debt management, multiple streams of income, and lifestyle stewardship are three keys to finding financial freedom.

The second category on the wheel is under the name financial foresight: being able to take care of business in view of what we see ahead of us. The first spoke for your assessment is asset protection. Asset protection deals with the

---

[68]Interview with Mark Victor Hansen, author of *Chicken Soup for the Soul* series, in February 2009 *Success from Home* magazine, 78ff.

fact that there are too many hands in our pockets. We have bureaucrats whose job is to get their hands deeper in our pockets legally and our job is to have them take as little out as possible legally. This is not being against government or against paying taxes. That is the legitimate expense of living in a civilized society.[69] The problem is that increased government bureaucracy does not solve our financial problems. Many of these fine people are simply paid to study problems in committees. The end result is we are finding ourselves having less and less ability to keep what little we are making.

The question I have for each of us today is what software or what advice are you utilizing to protect your assets. There are a lot of great programs out there. I want to mention another one, called "You Deduct," which comes as part of a Biz Pack software system that is now available on the market.[70] In "You Deduct" you are able to analyze over one hundred tax write offs that you may be able to qualify for with your small business, your home business, your multiple income stream, or to be able to ethically, legally, and legitimately take some hands out of your pockets to keep more of what you make and to protect your assets for you and your children's children beyond that.

The other group to learn from and to provide an alternative to is our consumer reliance on the banking system. We need banks for commercial purposes but there is a viable and creative way to become your own banker and accelerate both your protection and financial freedom at the same time.

---

[69]Kiyosaki, *Increase Your Financial IQ*, 52.
[70]For more information, contact www.u1stfinancial.net/equityforming.

There are various approaches to this, called "Be Your Own Banker," "Bank On Yourself," and the "Banker's Table" with the "BOSS" system.[71] This involves purchasing a quality whole life insurance policy from the most reputable companies. However, there are a mere handful out of the 1500 life insurance companies that offer the very specific policies that are dividend-paying whole life, provide a flexible paid-up additions rider, non-direct recognition (so your policy grows at the same rate when you borrow against your cash value), and have a great long-term track record of paying dividends while remaining strong financially.[72]

I have been using this method since 1994 with good results. What we are saying is that it is not financially intelligent to simply put your money in a bank savings account. Financial intelligence means to park our money in a place that it will be protected while also putting our money at the right place at the right time and the right amount for the right return. Today there are unprecedented tools that will help us to protect our assets.

The second spoke in the financial foresight quadrant is budgeting: to assess yourself on understanding how satisfied you are with the way you are approaching budgeting. A budget is your plan for the coordination of resources and expenditures. A budget is there because it is so much easier to spend money then to make it and many people are operating

---

[71]See www.infinitebanking.org, *Bank On Yourself: The Life Changing Secret to Protecting Your Financial Future* by Pamela Yellen (New York: Vanguard Press, 2009), and www.bankertable.com.
[72]Yellen, *Bank On Yourself,* 70.

on a budget deficit and they are borrowing to cover the cash flow deficit difference.

We know that the U.S. government has mortgaged the future because most government bureaucracies, no matter what political party, are designed to operate in a budget deficit. People may be appalled at what the government is doing, but we have created a climate for it because we are using our homes as an ATM machine and operating personally in the same way.

The key to budgeting is to make saving, giving, and investing areas in our life as a priority, not an option, but by listing them as a regular expense on our financial statements. In other words, it is not something we will get to someday, it is not a wish list, but we just build it right in. It may mean that we have to dial back on our lifestyle, on our ability to live a certain way. But if we start with 3 percent of our income allocated in our budget towards our assets, if its $1,000, we will be saving $30. The key is not where we start but that we start.

As we increase the percentages of our budget into our asset column, over time we are developing the higher achievement of acquiring greater financial intelligence. I know people whose dream is to live on 10 percent and give away 90 percent. It takes financial intelligence to be able to do that. But all of us can gain more intelligence so that we can be sure that we are budgeting in a way to protect our assets.

Foresight is also the ability to <u>leverage</u> our money, the next spoke in this quadrant. Simply stated, leveraging means doing more with less. We can easily recognize that $1 in a savings account has a leverage factor of 1:1 especially with the cost of living. But by leveraging other ways or even leveraging other people's money, we can get 1:4 and more leverage![73] That is what the money merge account and other creative software systems can help us achieve today.

As we increase our awareness and increase our financial intelligence we will be able to understand how best to leverage our money. Equity-forming Financial Coaching[74] has been established, along with Life-forming Leadership Coaching, to help you accelerate your FQ, with Equity-forming Financial Coaching enabling you to have the ability to understand how to leverage money and how to be in touch with coaches and financial planners who can help you best be both financially free and filled with financial foresight.

The next spoke in the foresight column is <u>learning</u>, simply defined as the ongoing financial education that we are committed to over our lives. We make fun of the agrarian-age thinking of generations ago; yet it still exists today. For instance, if our thinking is that land is the basis of all wealth that is certainly not proven to be the case in 2008 and beyond. Or if we cling to the industrial-age thinking that says, "I need a good job and a good education to get a higher paying job." But a good education may get us a job that is downsized. In the information-age thinking we do not need tangible resources but assessable information to solve our financial problems. This is the epitome of financial intelligence---learning where to get access to the kind of information that will solve our problems and increase our financial intelligence.

---

[73]Kiyosaki, *Increase Your Financial IQ*, 108 ff.

[74]See www.lifeformingcoach.com for information on financial lifestyle coaching.

We have looked at financial freedom, financial foresight, and now want to look at <u>financial fruitfulness</u> on the assessment wheel that we are calling financial intelligence. Financial fruitfulness begins with getting a <u>life focus</u>. Debt releasing is a key to dream realizing, but what are the dreams that you want to realize? Being able to sort that out with some coaching will help separate the wheat from the chaff and the daydreams from the destiny dreams. Being able to look at our lives in a way to get the cues and clues of what we are all about.

We have already referred to a study which showed 70 percent of executives had a glimpse of what they wanted to do in their life by the time they were in fourth grade. It seems that it is much more than a "one-time guess" but a lifetime confirmation of a focused life. When I heard about that study I began to ask those in fourth grade some key questions to anecdotally confirm that research. It provided me with some funny and compelling stories of where some of them thought they were heading! I am persuaded that a life focus that takes these early musings into account will make us more fruitful because it will enable us to learn to say "no" more often to the good and say "yes" emphatically to the best in our lives. So a life focus spoke is an important assessment piece to determine how focused you are in the dreams, in your sense of purpose, or your sense of what you are all about.

The second spoke under financial fruitfulness is <u>legacy</u>, which is all about the fact that we are to leave something more than what we've been given, including assets. This may be the first generation in which the children coming up will have less opportunity and assets than their parents. The Bible says that a good man leaves an inheritance to his children's children, so something has gone wrong in this generation.

105

My dad was a good man but he didn't leave me an inheritance. My father's dad was a good dad too, but he didn't leave him one. They were both cut off short in their lives without having protected their assets. As I've described earlier, my father had his rug pulled out from under him in terms of having all of his eggs in one basket---a single stream of income. I believe that having a good name is a legacy, the good relationships that we have with people is a legacy, and good assets are a legacy. For our focus here, it is important for us to assess what kind of legacy we are leaving for our children and our children's children.

Finally, we have the spoke that we are calling <u>poverty/philanthropy</u>. This is the ability for us to give, to invest, and to be able to have a part in helping people help themselves. The only thing that separates us from the poorest of the poor around the world is what latitude or longitude we happen to be born in, because many people are born in circumstances beyond their control. They only need a philanthropist to help them to get to the first rung of the ladder,[75] but from there on they can fulfill the bumper sticker slogan that declares: "I fight poverty, I work." There is some partial truth in that phrase. The full truth is that there is a good deal of people who want work but can't get to the first rung of work based on their circumstances, injustices, or lot in life. Our consistent giving to churches and charities will mean as much to us as to those who receive and steward these funds to help others here and around the world.

Once we recognize that we have an opportunity to become fruitful in these terms, we are really redefining

[75]See Jeffrey Sachs, *The End of Poverty: Economic Possibilities for Our Time* (new York: Penguin Group, 2005)..

success. Success from this FQ perspective is not how many toys we can accumulate but a legacy that we can leave of a life of focused living. It is the ability to help others get their first start, fresh start, or to get a jump start on a part of their lives that they are not going to get without the fruitfulness that comes from those of us who will invest in them and will be philanthropic towards them. So financial freedom, financial foresight, and financial fruitfulness is part of financial intelligence that will carry us effectively to the summits of our mountains and enable us to have, not just the wealth of money, but the wealth of access in our mountains, and the wealth of influence. FQ is a key to our destiny on the mountains.

CHAPTER SEVEN
CULTURAL INTELLIGENCE

Culture Wheel CQ
Transformational Intelligences for Home and Work©

CULTURAL INTELLIGENCE - CQ

It is attributed to Confucius, the saying, "He that knows one culture knows no culture." My interpretation of this wisdom is that it takes an intentional intelligence in other cultures to understand the strengths and weaknesses of your own. For this to play itself out in our paradigm we need to increase our intelligence culturally in order for us to be at our best in our own culture.

Cultural intelligence, or CQ, is a newly coined term offered in this series on transformational "intels." The cultural we are describing is in two areas. Certainly it is the culture of the geography where we live and work, including the culture of the organization in which we are operating. It is also the sensitivity to the dynamic mix of people in which we are working with: the multicultural, multi-ethnic, multi-generational, multi-gender, blend we are privileged to labor

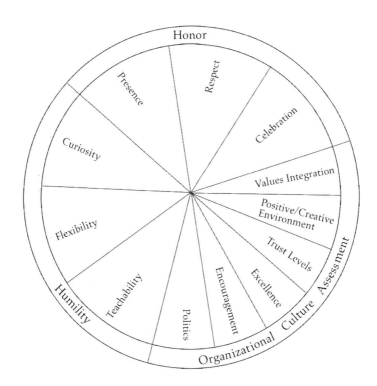

with. The ability to be intelligent culturally today is no longer an option. It is a key to success in the workplace. Our CQ wheel offers three areas of cultural intelligence. We are calling them organizational culture awareness, honor, and humility.

Let us begin with organizational culture awareness and what we mean by that topic. Organizational culture awareness is the ability to answer the question, "How do things really work around here?" It is an important issue because we want to know that no matter how we work, or how someone we are working with chooses to work, there is a culture of an organization that we can either hinder or enhance. Depending on where the company, school, or organization may be operating, there is a certain environment or culture in that community where most of the people have a certain work ethic, frame of reference, world-view, and way of looking at life. Not taking that into account is a highway for disappointment.

I remember one individual who was a great worker in a company here, and he would work late at night and he would sleep-in, as was his norm. He then moved to one particular farm community out of state where most of the people had an ethic of early to rise. They were up at four o'clock in the morning, milking the cows or doing other things, and they never saw his lights on in the morning. By the time he felt he had settled in, the rumor was out and set in stone that he was lazy; and probably must be on some kind of welfare program. He had a very difficult time from then on in that culture because he did not have the awareness of what the community expected, even unwritten expectations, as an irreducible minimum standard of behavior.

We need to become more aware of the importance of cultural intelligence in our geographic and organizational environment or ethos. With that awareness we want to have a role in creating what I am calling a "culture of honor."[76] Great ideas go nowhere if the culture is not receptive. Culture has been called the shared software of our minds.[77] In other words, like our processing software in our computers, people have a way of thinking or a way of handling things or data that is a coded, shared concept in any organization. In order to shift culture where we live and work to be more creative and excellent, I believe it is significantly determined by how we honor others in that culture, especially as we approach culture with a humility posture.

These three areas of awareness, honor, and humility are starting blocks to operate in the multicultural environment, the corporate environment, and the organizational environments that are required today. We are not just targeting international corporations with CQ, but also local and global, where we operate in ways that express cultural intelligence. We recognize also that we are not only looking to understand the concept but to shift the environments we work in through the concept of CQ.

The first spoke under organizational culture awareness is what we are calling <u>values integration</u>.[78]

---

[76]See footnote discussion from chapter eight on relational intelligence.

[77]See Wayne Cordeiro and Robert Lewis, *Culture Shift: Transforming Your Church from the Inside Out* (San Francisco: Jossey-Bass, 2005).

[78]See Audrey Malphurs, *Values-Driven Leadership: Discovering and Developing Your Core Values for Ministry* (Grand Rapids: Baker Books, 2004). My doctoral students over the years have made significant changes, both personal and organizational, as a result of his breakdown of this topic of values integration.

Assessing by this category targets questions regarding how the culture of your organization personifies its values. In other words, "Does the way things work around here personify the very values that are on paper or have been a part of the founder's intentions?" Another key question is, "Does the organization behave accordingly to those values?" A more penetrating question is, "Does the organization treat people both inside and out in alignment with the beliefs it espouses?"[79] Simply put, is there an integration of values in the way that we treat people, inside and out? This is an important starting point for us to have. We need to be aware of what exists before we can shift that culture in a healthy way and know specifically how to honor that culture no matter what "givens" we face.

The second spoke is the ability to have a positive/creative environment. The question here is, "Does the organization emit a positive climate that attracts outsiders and encourages insiders to fulfill their role in the mission?" People want to be on board. People do not leave jobs, they leave relationships, and too often it is because the climate within that organization is such that the relationships are not healthy. We want people who are attracted to being part of the team and once they are in, to stay motivated to fulfill the mission of that team or organization.[80]

---

[79]Crafting penetrating questions is a skill that can be quickly acquired and can have a long lasting impact. See the authors on-line Real Talk Training, described at www.lifeformingcoach.com.

[80]The largest cost savings that a company can have is the reduced cost of employee training that comes from worker satisfaction and low turnover. See the excellent book, *The Dream Manager* by Matthew Kelly (New York: Beacon Publishing, 2007), describing this difference.

"Is there an atmosphere that encourages individuality, creativity, risk taking, innovation, mutual respect, and team work?" In other words, climate or atmosphere makes the difference. An atmosphere that stifles or an atmosphere that stimulates is a key role of CQ for an organizational culture awareness. We need a new breed of culturally intelligent workers, leaders, and owners who are able to take the pulse and then be able to apply the remedy. In CQ the positive, creative organizational climate is critical towards the other factors in this "intel" wheel.

The third spoke in this category is called <u>trust levels</u>. To assess trust in your organization, we must ask, "Does the organizational climate nurture healthy, interpersonal relationships? Do the leaders trust each other and their employees? Does the organizational culture serve to build high trust levels?" There is no doubt about it that old-fashioned trust goes a long way to overlook a multitude of mistakes and to create an atmosphere where people can risk and to give their best. Though hard to assess,[81] it certainly is easy to pick up when it is not there.

The fourth spoke in the area of organizational <u>culture</u> awareness is assessing the environment for producing <u>excellence</u>. Some professional teams have created such cultures that caused players to note that just by putting on their uniforms makes them motivated to give their best! Some appropriate questions for assessing this area include: "Does the organizational culture encourage and sustain standards of

---

[81]Life-forming Leadership Coaching administers two excellent assessment instruments: the *Winslow Personality Profile* and the *Mind Scan,* that help measure personal and group trust levels. See www.lifeformingcoach.com.

excellence? Is it really part of the ethos to want to be excellent and the ability to sustain that? Does the organizational culture put a value on quality and continuous improvement? Does it celebrate high standards of development in all the workers from their character to their productivity?"

The fifth spoke in this large category is one with a common name, but with an uncommon occurrence: encouragement. This trait can be expressed in several ways, but can best be measured by the life-giving quality of the staff or project meetings that are either the blessing or the curse of any organization.[82] Some appropriate questions here might be: "Does the organizational culture sincerely encourage or simply offer pep rallies? How does the encouragement fit the individual as compared to a 'one size fits all' approach? What stories are told in how the role of encouragement has played a key part in the life of the organization?"

The final spoke in the area of organizational culture awareness is the politics of the organization. Politics and politicking are a way of life wherever people and departments vie for limited resources. As we assess any cross-currents of agendas and purposes within the organization, our awareness of the role of politics in the organization can be sharpened by the following questions: "Are there internal struggles for control in various areas? Are interpersonal conflicts resolved satisfactorily? How does a newcomer break into any 'old boy club' circles?"

---

[82]See Patrick Lencioni, *Death by Meeting: A Leadership Fable...About Solving the Most Painful Problem in Business* (San Francisco: Jossey-Bass, 2004)..

The questions offered in this organizational culture awareness area can be asked for an individual's assessment or they can be used in a 360-degree approach by anonymously asking the same question to various constituencies within the organization. They are simple, but laser-like attempts to help us assess the organizational climate and evaluate the positive creative atmosphere, the trust levels, the excellence levels, and the political levels. As we apply these kinds of questions to the organization, we will become more culturally intelligent in understanding what we are currently dealing with and how applying that awareness is able to bring about organizational transformation.

After twelve years of training coaches in over twenty-three countries in eleven languages, we believe in the unique dynamic of coaching to enhance CQ.[83] Organizational coaching provides leaders with methods of identifying organizational constraints and then provides a relational coaching process of addressing them in a healthy life-giving way. Simply stated, it is about identifying anything in an organization that is holding back creativity or excellence.

In creating new culture awareness, we are more able to shift that culture to strategic thinking, planning, implementation, and feedback, so that any leader can begin to identify a logjam or a bottleneck and initiate internal transformation. It is inevitable that every organization will need renewing or revitalization. The foundation for that is

---

[83]One international hotel chain has moved closer to being tops in customer service, in part due to a contract with us in which we trained 440 managers and 4,400 staff around some of the issues in CQ and EQ.

CQ. For intelligent encouragement, we need to culturally understand how things really work around here.

The second area on our wheel is the ability to <u>honor</u> people within the culture. When we talk about honor we mean giving the gift of honor to another.[84] The first spoke in this area of CQ is assessing our level of competence regarding <u>presence.</u> This defines how present we are to others in any organization, but also how present we are to others who are from any other culture in terms of our cultural intelligence. Presence means to be able to listen to people, especially when they are coming from another perspective, world-view, religious paradigm, and cultural way of dressing, acting, or eating.

Listening is a key to being present. "To listen," means to be trained to listen at levels two and three.[85] Celebrating how each of us being fearfully and wonderfully made includes honoring how each of us is designed and motivated to listen. These many include any of five different listening styles that we or another prefer,[86] as well as cultural styles of communication that are added layers to the listening process.

I will never forget a gentleman who I never met before and was to pick him up at a restaurant. He was quite a well-known consultant, and I was thinking about the small talk I will have for the twenty-minute chauffeuring drive in which I

---

[84]For a visual demonstration between how cultures honor, simply compare the way you are treated as a customer on an Asian airline and an American airline.

[85]Level one is, "What does this mean to me?" Level two is, "What do they mean by this?" Level three is, "What does this mean to them?"

[86]See Inscape Publishing, *Personal Listening Profile* at http://www.internalchange.com.

would be conversing with him regarding the history of our area. Before I could introduce myself in the restaurant, he stood up and reached out his hand and said, "I have been reading about you on the Internet. Do you mind if I ask you a question?" I was prepared for the historical questions common to my area of the country but not for what he asked me next.

He then asked, "If you keep doing in the next five years what you have been doing the last, where will you be in terms of your dreams and goals?" I was rather taken aback by a stranger jumping right in to that level. What surprised me even more was my response. I actually told him of my frustrated dreams and work situation and I was surprised how I felt so easy to do so with someone I had just met. Twenty minutes later, after I dropped him to his destination, I began a three-month reflection about that conversation.

What he did was simply ask me a powerful question that caused me to reflect and align. He had such a presence in that twenty minutes that I felt like I knew him all my life. He listened to what really mattered in my response and then asked me another question. At the end of twenty minutes, all he had done was ask me probably about five to eight questions that gave me the ability to begin to align my life around my design, desires, dream, and destiny. Now, ten years later, I am producing these "intel" assessments for you so that you are able to align the way you live and the way you work.

The key to this story was that it began with someone who honored me. He was from a different culture and he stepped into my world with such a sense of presence, by listening, asking, and helping me to reflect and learn in a way that I am deeply grateful for that turning point conversation. It also taught me that we are always only one conversation away from a breakthrough either to us or through us where we live and work. The whole purpose of these intelligences, especially this one on the cultural intelligence, is for us to see many more breakthroughs rather than breakdowns when it comes to our multicultural communications.

Unfortunately, Americans are known around the world for having somewhat of an arrogant, monocultural, monolingual tendency to project demands on others of what they have come to expect back home, whether it is restaurant, service, or business communications. The old phrase "the ugly American" is easily discovered in travels around the world when we observe the way others treat people one on one. To have the cultural intelligence of honor means to be present to people and to listen, learn, ask more rather than tell and demand, and reflect on the quality of our interactions because the "quality of our conversations is a measure of the quality of our relationships."[87]

The second spoke under the category of honoring people and creating a culture of honor organizationally is respect: R-e-s-p-e-c-t. This famous spelled-out phrase, from the recording by Aretha Franklin, is worth hearing regularly so that we are aware of the need to assess how we are communicating respect to others, especially from different cultures. Respect means to recognize diversity in others, not to just glaze over it. Saying, "Well, I do not even see your skin color," is an affront to people. There is nothing more important than respecting another by being able to take note

---

[87] I attribute this great statement to Marie, my wife of forty years, a tireless fighter for a great marriage with great communication, and my role model for this area of my life.

of their uniqueness in ways they feel honored or prized. They will feel respected when we do so in a positive way.[88]

We give respect by giving room for culturally significant moments. In other words, we make room in our lives, in our relationships, in the multicultural environment in which we work, to have someone express a significant moment in their life. These may be a right of transition for them or their family, a special day that is celebrated in their faith community or in their nation back home, or whatever is important to them that may not be part of our lives. Respecting others is to recognize that diversity by giving room for that significant moment to be expressed, to be talked about, and to be validated.

The third spoke under honoring others with CQ is to celebrate. When we say celebrate we mean celebrate, not tolerate. Toleration may be a great American virtue, but it is not very intelligent when it comes to working with people on your mountain in the workplace. People want to be celebrated and not tolerated. We need to give the gift of public honor, public affirmation, public validation, and public esteem. There is nothing better than to feel prized, singled out, and that you are important. We do that by not just recognizing people's achievement, which is a standard expectation in the workplace, but to celebrate who they are and their uniqueness, and to honor their diverse contribution and perspective.

We need an ability to increase our cultural intelligence rapidly if we are going to be relevant. "To be irrelevant is to

---

[88]Years of work to establish multiethnic churches have been a real proving ground for this chapter.

be irreverent"[89] as author Mark Batterson likes to say. We don't want to be irreverent to anyone's culture or to his or her religion. We want to be relevant to the fact that we can be intentionally pleasant to people, respect, and celebrate them. This is the kind of gift of honor in the workplace that will shift an organizational climate to one of creativity and excellence.

The third area on the CQ wheel is good old-fashioned humility. Humility is a key when it comes to cross-cultural interactions, and to be able to understand the environments in which we operate. Humility is a choice, a posture, not some kind of weakness or withdrawal. You can be very strong, but very humble.

Humility involves the spoke called curiosity. Curiosity is a sense of awe and wonder at life and the desire to simply learn something new every day in every relationship. In a sense it's a rediscovery of a childlikeness we have lost along the way. Not that we are childish, but to come back to what we had as children when we continually wanted to know. We were curious. We didn't even have an agenda to fix people or to get them to be like us; we just wanted to know why this and why that. We were observant; we were trying to figure out life. We can recapture that. And the curiosity to know, to ask curious questions, and to come alongside people, tells them we have an interest in them. It disarms others to know that we are taking a posture wherein we don't know everything about their culture, we don't know everything about them, and we think it's worth the time and effort to know.

---

[89]This quote came from Mark Batterson in a conference in 2007, and is part of his core values for the work he is doing in Washington. D.C., found in www.theaterchurch.com.

One of the greatest mistakes of a colonial attitude in business, education, or religion is the missed opportunities that have come from a cultural illiteracy.[90] Until we know another culture, and are curious and humble enough to investigate it, we really don't know our own culture in view of the strengths, weaknesses, prejudices, and the achievements that are unique to it. We really don't know ours until we take time to know theirs.

The second aspect of humility is flexibility. This is the willingness for us to be flexible in a learning environment in which there is a multicultural aspect. Cultural intelligence is a key to the global economy, even the newly termed "glocal" economy, because the global is now local. Flexibility in the context of CQ means that we should focus on personal assessment. It also requires a focus on policy assessment for the organization. Flexibility means we are willing to bend policies to understand how people can best fit in.

Policies are usually made by good people who unknowingly make them from their limited monocultural perspective. To add more fuel to the fire, it then grows to become company policy to enforce that policy rather than flex it. But company policy is about company and company is people. Policy has to fit the people that make it up.

The ability to be flexible is a great mark of humility. To be able to say; "You know it may have worked then, but one size doesn't fit all now. We want some tailor-made ability to address the opportunities and the needs of our people today." This posture in the workplace says we are lifelong learners, and "the biggest room in the house is always the room for

---

[90]From a lecture at Regent University by Dr. Howard Foltz, 2004.

improvement." This includes the way an organization is flexible enough to embrace the diversity that makes it up.

The final spoke of humility is what I call teachability. The best way to summarize it is our eagerness to learn something new from anyone and everyone. I see this need whenever a student comes to see me as a professor and tries to flatter me with an emphasis on my title, only to discover that when they left my office and turned the corner they treated a janitor or a worker with disdain in their tone of voice. What they don't realize is that they can learn as much from a janitor as they can learn from a professor.

Teachability means that we have a lifelong learning posture. There are nuggets of gold in every day's encounters, in every day's relationships, in every day's conversations. The ability to keep track of some of these "learnings" separates the women from the girls and the men from the boys in the realm of CQ. Every person can be your teacher, every experience can deepen your learning and forward your development, but it only happens when we are humble enough to realize that it can come from the strangest places, from the most unrecognized perspectives in people from different cultural expressions.

When we are humble, curious, flexible, and teachable we can honor others by becoming the kind of culturally intelligent people who do not just "get 'er done" on the job, but cause the workplace environment to be creative and productive. Transformational intelligences begin and end with these seven and beyond, but for the sake of culturally intelligent leaders and workers, the time is now, and the time is more pertinent than ever to apply these to our lives.

CHAPTER EIGHT
RELATIONAL INTELLIGENCE

Relational Wheel   RQ
Transformational Intelligences for Home and Work©

RELATIONAL INTELLIGENCE ⅃ RQ

Though it could be called the social networking quotient, we are going to make it a shorter title and name the next "intel" the relational quotient, or <u>relational intelligence</u>. Depending on how we frame this discussion is how we will best understand its impact. On your assessment wheel you will see three rather strange phrases that you probably have never heard before or seen put together. The first one is <u>personal relational equity</u>, the second one is <u>relational change influence</u>, and the third one is <u>glocal relational alignment</u>. I understand that this discussion may be a hard one to pull off, just understanding why we would use those complicated words, but it is really not that complicated. In fact, it is an expressive way for us to assess what really matters in each of these.

Joseph L. Umidi

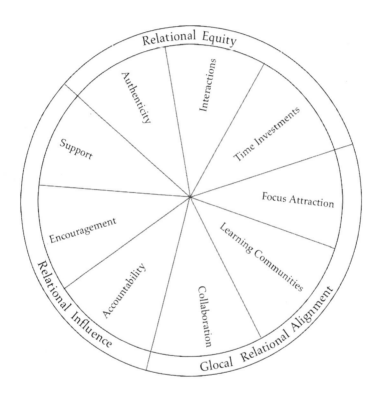

Personal relational equity is what we have and what we invest when it comes to relational intelligence; building up a bank account, so to speak, of the way that we invest in others. Sometimes we have to withdraw from the bank, but we need to have something to withdraw from. This simply means that over a period of time we are investing in relationships. Understanding the role of personal relational equity is a key to relational intelligence.

The first spoke in this section of the wheel is called catalyzing authenticity.[91] People are looking for the real deal. They want people to be real and are not too impressed with corporate hype, political spin, or religious talk. They want real talk, they want real people, they want authenticity, and they want us to be seen in what we are like off the PowerPoint presentation, and off the platform. They would like to have a water cooler conversation with us, not just a public presentation.

Authenticity is a key part of relational equity. To be authentic means to be willing to tell the whole story, not just the story that makes you look good, but also the story that makes you look real. In other words, it is to be intentional about the fact that all of us are a work in progress and no one is impressed any longer with the image only, "fake it until you make it" or "there is no business like show business and even when you are brokenhearted, the show must go on." That may have worked in the boomer generation□ it may still work

---

[91]This is a core part of the coach training offered in either the formation or accelerated coach training tracks that enable a student to receive the growth coach credential which opens up a wide array of income opportunities. Contact info@lifeformingcoach.com for more information.

in some of the corporate world□ but what will impress people today is the fresh air, the aroma of someone who actually is more real than some ideal. To be that way enables us to actually catalyze it in others. In other words, when we determine that we are secure enough in who we are, we are able to tell a joke on ourselves, be more self-effacing, or we are able to laugh at our own mistakes because we are not failures; we just fail forward.[92] To have that kind of security, identity, or even humor about it creates in others a desire for it as well. That is why we say it is catalyzing authenticity.

The assessment spoke called personal relational equity is about how competent we are at being able to catalyze authenticity at the office, or in a conversation with another. This ability causes people to relax, to disarm their defenses so to speak, whether you are a manager, supervisor, staff, board member, employee, or whatever role you may have. When you have RQ it will cause people to feel they can connect with you. No matter what title you have, or what you have accomplished in the past, you are accessible and approachable in their eyes. Relational equity starts with modeling being real and because of that, being able to catalyze authenticity in that relationship.

Organizations may be resistant to authenticity, and, in fact, may actually have an entitlement mentality. This means the focus is mostly on what the management or what the worker can get for themselves much more than a concern for others. The role of RQ enables anyone to ignite and catalyze authenticity, when we have developed to a place of caring

---

[92]See John C. Maxwell, *Failing Forward: Turning Mistakes into Stepping Stones for Sucess* (Nashville: Thomas Nelson, 2007), for an excellent treatment of this in his book.

more about others and the context in which we live out our lives than about ourselves. Those organizations that have evolved to greatness over decades and even generations have operated at a high level of relational intelligence, especially in this area of authenticity, which breeds transparency and trust.[93]

The second spoke is what we are calling <u>maximize personal interactions</u>. Every one of us has interaction opportunities each day but are we intentional about maximizing the impact of those so that they can accumulate the relational equity over a period of time? That means instead of just treating our interactions casually, we actually are more intentional about getting the most from them. Sometimes this means preparing for them ahead of time. One of the ways to do that is to learn to ask great questions.[94] The ability to help move a stranger into an acquaintance, an acquaintance into a friendship, or a friendship into a partnership is in the art of maximizing personal interactions through great questions.

What I have confirmed over the last twelve years through conversation workshops around the world is that questions, more than statements, are a great way to maximize personal time with people. It accelerates our ability to get to know them and draw out of them the ability to share with us something that is important to them, something that is

---

[93]See Jim Collins, *Good to Great* (New York: HarperCollins Publishing, 2001), for classic research described in his book.

[94]See the bibliography near the end of this book for a list of helpful books on this subject. One key to note is that it is more than the technology of what you ask. It is more about how you ask with a heart posture that believes in another and is genuinely interested in their unique development.

significant, or something that is a challenge. Preparing to maximize these interactions we will have throughout the day means thinking through crafting a couple of questions that go beyond small talk, shop talk, busy talk, or idle talk, and actually go to a creative talk, real talk, even what we call breakthrough talk: people being able to breakthrough to a new meaning or a new appreciation.[95] That comes by intentionally saying to our self, "I am going to make the best use. I am going to maximize my personal interactions so that I can increase my relational equity, and, as a result, become more relationally intelligent."

The third spoke under personal relational equity is <u>time investment.</u> Time investment simply says the way that we spell love at home is t-i-m-e, not just the quality time, but it is quantity time. As we apply relational intelligence to the home first, before any of our vocational mountains, we recognize that certain times are more important than others for critical results. Time over a meal table, or "table talk," is the willingness to make time to eat together. Time for life learning or "teachable moment" time is to be available when our family is most likely to want to have conversations. Late at night when we tuck them in creates certain key moments for heart-to-heart connections. These are the ways to invest our time wisely.

---

[95]The one exercise in the Real Talk Training that has had the biggest effect is helping people craft a few penetrating questions in preparation for an important conversation they will be having in the short term. Feedback has been overwhelmingly positive in over twenty-three countries, that being intentional with questions make a big difference.

Some investments yield bigger returns and the right kind of time investment for our family will yield some of the best memories and the best milestones in our lives that make our family life stories worth modeling by others. Of course, at work our time investments will operate in a different environment. For instance, we can maximize time when we are going to do something by intentionally including other people. We still have to do the event, still have to have the meal, still have to do the traveling, but how might we in a wide sense of stewardship of our time include the ability to develop personal relational equity with another in that event that has to take place? That is operating in personal relational equity, the first key to relational intelligence.

The second key to RQ we are calling <u>relational change influence</u>, again three words rarely put together. This is the ability to help people to reach momentum in their lives, even sustainable momentum. We discovered in our application of the "wave theory" of change[96] that in order for people to make major changes in their lives, they need the ability to have people who are coming alongside with their influence, putting their shoulder with them in the process of helping them to get to the next level and to stay at that level.

The illustration would be if you want a pot of water to boil and you are in a hurry, the choice of simply waiting is not an option. Your obvious choice is to turn up the heat. When you turn it up from 209 to 210 it may only require one calorie or one unit of heat to get one degree of difference. When you go

---

[96]Our sustainable change model in training is derived from this model of language change popularized by William Labov, "Transmission and Diffusion," Journal of the Luingistic Society of America 83, no. 2 (June 2007).

from 210 to 211, another calorie, another unit of energy is required if you cannot wait. But when you go from 211 to 212, something happens to the water as it begins to boil and the water has a major phase change from water to vapor. It requires more than one unit of energy; at least seventy. The implication for us in change influence is that anybody is capable of making minor changes along the way. But if our work associates, our family, or our friends want to make a major phase change in their life, they need more sustainable energy applied to them to get them to the place where they can make that transition. We are calling these the three spokes of support, encouragement, and accountability.

The first spoke is <u>support</u> and that is the ability to put our efforts, thoughts, creative thinking, and time to a person or a team that really wants to get to a new level of performance, or a new level of operation or significance. We are supporting them in that endeavor. We are saying, "We are here for you; in fact, we are going to set aside some time, we are going to set aside some quality resources, but most of all, we are putting our shoulder to it, and you can count on us to help you get the big momentum up and going." Support is very meaningful. It is tangible, people can feel it, it involves time, can involve money, but most of all, it involves the ability to be present, to be engaged, and to be in the moment with people. It is the ability to plan for that contingency in our day so that people can actually know that it is a tangible support. It is not "if you need me," but "hey here I am, what do you need me to do?"

The second spoke, we are calling <u>encouragement.</u> Encouragement is particularly important during times of discouragement. Encouragement is "just in time;" it is a "word that is fitly spoken."[97] It is a word that sustains people when they feel like they are ready to throw in the towel. Encouragement is best appreciated when it is given at the time most needed. It is not just "attaboy," "attagirl;" encouragement is actually the ability to give people courage, and it usually comes because people can feel that we are with them.[98] We have a similar energy that we are applying to them when they are at their lowest. It is pictured in the river that is rising and it looks like it is going to flood the homes, and just in time here comes the encouragement with the workers with the sandbags to be able to build it up another five feet to protect the homes from overflow.

Encouragement means we are picking up the early warning detection signals that somebody needs to be encouraged. Perhaps the encouragement could be in helping them to recover the reason or the vision of the project, or perhaps to align themselves with the "why" of their doing it, the values behind it, or the values they want to live by. However we define it, the end result is the ability to attach our motivation and energy to someone when they are at their lowest, empty, or drain point. Just in time to provide support and encouragement helps people get past the common "one step forward and two steps back." It helps them to begin to enjoy sustainable progress and momentum.

The third part of this three-fold cord is <u>accountability</u>. Notice, we put the accountability spoke third and not first. In fact, accountability is not healthy when it is on its own.

---

[97]Quoted from the Bible, Prov. 25:11.
[98]See Scott, *Fierce Conversations*, for great illustrations of support, encouragement, and accountability through conversations in the workplace.

Accountability needs to be connected to support and encouragement. Accountability is the ability to hold people accountable, mostly to what they said they wanted to do, what they agreed to, what they signed up for, or what goals they said yes to. It is not accountability necessarily to us. It is accountability to their "yes," to what all they have said they wanted to do. Simply to remind them of that, what they said they were willing to do, what they agreed to have us ask them about, can change everything. To have a system in which they have agreed in advance to wanting to be accountable to that process enables us to offer accountability without being toxic,[99] controlling, and without being demeaning. Healthy accountability is done in the context of healthy support and healthy encouragement. Relational change influence is saying that RQ is evidenced when we are able to receive and give support, encouragement, and accountability to people who want a significant phase change in their personal or organizational life.

The last category in RQ is another unique combination of words that begins with the word "glocal." Glocal is a combination of global and local, and it means that we need to be operating on both levels in this era of time. We need to have RQ with people that we are around daily and with the people who are on the same pursuit, path, or vocational mountain as we are, many of them connected globally or

---

[99]Toxic leadership is the opposite of a healthy EQ and RQ and needs to be kept in check by healthy appeal or grievance procedures in place and in good working order. Every leader needs another peer or mentor/coach to be sure they are learning from the times in which they have used their positional authority at the expense of their relational equity.

regionally, especially through the Internet and through the modern technology that we all possess today. There is certainly a huge shift that has happened. There is a social media available today that has never been available before. There are places on the Internet that allow us to be social, to be relational, and to interact. Whether it is YouTube, Twitter, MySpace, Facebook, LinkedIn, or blogging, we can attract people to us when we talk about the things that people are interested in.

The ability to operate intelligently in this media, this environment today, is a critical factor in our ability to have access to success in our mountain. Web 2.0 is the second generation of Web. It was 1996 when the Internet started, and it is as if there is a revolution now that started in this Web 2.0; it is a massive movement. In the previous version you had to be technical, you had to be a geek, but now, you do not need any of that to be able to have access globally and locally to what we are calling a <u>glocal relational alignment</u>. Aligning ourselves with people that have similar interests, similar desires to help each other, to learn from each other, and then adding this second generation of easier-to-use Internet to socialize in a nontechnical way, to connect, is really where people are and where they are going. Make no doubt about it.

Facebook saw an 89 percent increase in unique visitors from May 2006 to May 2007. MySpace has accumulated 67 million members since its launch in 2004. LinkedIn is growing rapidly, pulling in 361 percent more unique visitors that it did in 2007. YouTube has more than 100 million videos served daily less than two years after launch. EBay in the first quarter of 2009 traded $8 billion and is on track to trade $32 billion. Amazon hired 500 staff and its traffic trends show acceleration while commerce around them outside the Internet is showing deterioration. [100] This is an incredible explosion that we are seeing around us in terms of this revolution of ability to connect socially and relationally in ways that are unheard of in the past, while giving us the ability to go global as well as local.

In this global relational alignment, the first spoke is collaboration. We want to collaborate with others in our pursuits, to share information and resources over the Internet through these social needs so that we can jump over traditional ways of locking out information and access. There is a wealth of access and a wealth of influence that has come because of this glocal relational alignment. Aligning ourselves with others in our similar profession or similar pursuits will enable us to have an exponential impact in areas that, up to this date, were impossible but for a few elite. Access yourself in terms of collaboration.

How are you collaborating with others through Web 2.0? Are you satisfied with your present level of learning? In the last few months, I've been coached in the area of being able to understand how to operate in the Web 2.0 environments and it has changed my life. I assessed myself and found myself engaging a coach in the process. As a result, I am very satisfied with what I'm learning and with what I see coming in my own career calling as a result of this great collaboration I'm having with others. Aligning myself relationally with some key players around the world in the very thing I'm interested in has been the joy of collaboration.

---

[100]Statistics taken from the unpublished business plan proposal for Get2Marketing by Christian Redshaw, June 2009.

The second spoke is <u>learning communities</u>. This is a key factor for us because what we have discovered is that information does not bring transformation. Transformation is more a product of motivation.[101] What motivates us is to be in a learning environment or "learning community" in which we are sparking each other; we are providing an atmosphere that resonates with a hunger to learn. Here we will learn more, we will learn faster, and we will maintain our learning longer because we are learning together.[102] This learning community means blogging, interacting, and the ability to give ourselves to that process on a regular basis. If we are too busy to blog, we are really too busy to be doing business.

Interacting with others is simply being part of a learning community in which we are spending simply one half hour a day interacting in a learning environment over some topic. By participating, giving, and receiving, and simply blogging around a particular area in our profession, we will bring relational intelligence to many because of the relational dynamics of a learning community.

---

[101]This phrase refers to the alignment of knowledge with our why for that knowledge: values, passions, dreams, legacy, survival, and urgency. Without engaging the process to discover the "pain or pleasure" connected to the knowledge, there is little transformation that integrates knowledge with the full dimensions of our unique design.

[102]After research on master teachers the author has concluded that the weaknesses of the formal method must be corrected with the addition of the nonformal relational mentoring and coaching. A close study of the teaching role of Jesus Christ revealed that he paid more attention to the "context" of the training/learning; i.e., the learning community, than the "content" of the training. The end result was and is transformational.

The final spoke is <u>focused attraction</u>. This means that the more we are putting forth the things we are learning in this open-sourced atmosphere, not being afraid of the competition, but simply being a part of the abundance of this global relational alignment worldwide with people, the more we will attract others to us and our mission. The more we put out there what we are learning and struggling with, the more attraction there will be with others who are in the same place at the same time, even though they may be in a different geographical area. We become like a magnet and a filter. In other words, we filter out those who don't have the time or the interest, but we attract like a magnet those who are at the same place, just behind us, or just ahead of us, and will enable us all to advance on our mountain in a steady climb. Not just one step forward and two steps back, but to be able to occupy the ground that we cover, to be able to hold the territory we gain, to be able to get a secure footing and enjoy the view. That niche attraction will come because there is a relational intelligence we are developing that is being shared in the glocal community worldwide. Here is the wheel of relational intelligence. Let's assess ourselves and let's make sure that wheel is in alignment with the assignment in our lives.

CHAPTER NINE
VOCATIONAL INTELLIGENCE

Vocational Wheel - VQ
Transformational Intelligences for Home and Work©

VOCATIONAL INTELLIGENCE ♪ VQ

This section deals with the intelligence called "vocational intelligence" or VQ. We could have called this work intelligence, or some other name, but we want to point out these transformational intelligences can operate both personally and organizationally. In addition to whatever due diligence needs to be done in our vocation we also need a unique VQ. This is described in this wheel of vocational intelligence with three key sections: <u>preparation</u>, <u>perspiration,</u> and <u>inspiration.</u>

When we think about <u>preparation</u>, we recognize that in some sense there is a required standard of <u>education.</u> Education is part of the process of the culture we live in today, and there is a certain expectation in this first spoke that every person would have met an irreducible minimum standard of education that is required for anybody being in a

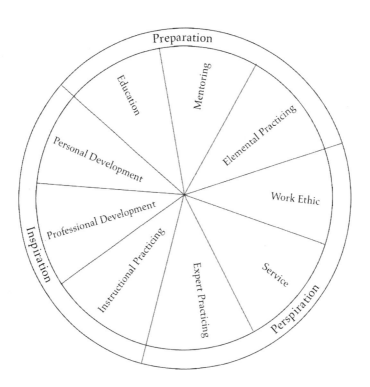

particular profession. As you assess yourself, think of your competency in terms of either the present level of education that you have, or the level of education that you need to be at the top of your game in your vocation. Education means the schooling, the ability to meet standardized scores, tests, or certifications that are required to pass those, whether they are bar exams, real estate exams, or whatever it takes. The education itself needs to be defined in terms of your specific profession, but there is a preparation that must be done and that process must be embraced.

The idea of being called to a profession means to express your best. It is not just getting the education over with so that you can do what you want to do, but it is embracing the educational process itself. Education is more than preparation; it has a lifelong aspect to it as well. Assess yourself regarding your present level of competency, perhaps as ongoing education on the educational spoke.

The second spoke is the word <u>mentoring</u>. Mentoring is an important piece because effective preparation for a vocation involves more than a classroom, and it certainly involves more than a textbook. It involves finding and being with the very people who are in the profession whom we are giving our lives to, especially the people who are at their best. The concept of mentoring here means there are multiple mentors we can have, both in the preparation process and when we transition into our profession itself.[103] The key is that they

---

[103]See Robert Clinton and Paul Stanley, *Connecting: The Mentoring Relationships You Need to Succeed* (Colorado Springs: NavPress Publishing Group, 1992), for a mentoring model that includes nine types of short-term mentors at various stages of our lives.

should be specific in their time and focus. If you approach someone and say, "Will you mentor me?" you can almost watch their eyes glaze over like deer in the headlights. Yet when we approach someone and say, "I am interested in having some influence from you in a specific area. Could you possibly meet with me once or twice a month for two or three months and help me to know how I can develop that area?" When we are specific with a person, with a request over an area for a specific amount of time, potential mentors do not see themselves as having to be a lifetime guru. Instead, they can have a limited time impact in an area that they have some competence and confidence, and they can evaluate whether they had the time for it now because you have made a specific request from them.

Mentoring evaluation is an important foundational conversation to have in order to insure we are able to finish well what we start in the mentoring relationship. Unfortunately, I have seen a number of mentoring relationships that started without that built-in process of evaluation and they ended worse than when they started. People who were acquaintances, or friends, or had some respect for each other before the mentoring process itself, ended up having a breakdown that caused them to avoid each other after the mentoring. In fact, they prematurely ended the mentoring feeling that there were expectations or assumptions which were not clarified, and they determined not to do it again. The way to avoid this is to have an upfront simple agreement with a built-in evaluation process, in which you can say at the end of the fourth or fifth meeting, "Let us evaluate how it is going, whether it needs to be adjusted, or if it needs to celebrate its ending."[104] In other words, a clear exit strategy can minimize something that could drag on and on. Preparation involves education, maybe formally, and it involves mentoring relationships that are multiple, specific, and evaluative.

Education also involves what I am calling here <u>practice in the elements</u>. What do I mean by that? None of us are going to be at our game, at our best, unless we do practice in the basic fundamentals. The famous phrase purportedly given by Vince Lombardi at the beginning of every season is, "This is a football." To these guys who had played football for years, he was basically saying, "We are going to be sure that we have the elements down, the basics of the blocking, and the tackling. We are going to practice until we have them and then we are going to re-practice them when we return again next season in order for us not to miss the foundation."

When you read about some of the most effective people in their careers, the most common denominator is sacrificial practice. Recent research shows there is at least 10,000 hours that a person has to put in to be at the top of his game.[105] In order for us to put in 10,000 hours over a period of time, we really have to enjoy the first 100 or the first 1,000 because if you do not like to practice, you will never be prepared. We have to practice, but we have to develop an attitude about it that causes us to see the end in the beginning, and to be willing to have mentors and others to help us get the foundations of the elements down. The first section is

---

[104]See the appendices in this book for a sample of this agreement.

[105]See Malcolm Gladwell, *Outliers: The Story of Success* (New York: Little, Brown and Company, 2008), chapter two.

preparation, assessing yourself regarding your level of satisfaction.

The second section is <u>perspiration</u>. Certainly there is perspiration in the preparation, but what do we mean by perspiration? We are talking here about a healthy <u>work ethic</u>. Depending on where you are coming from in this spectrum, this could be a loaded topic because you may think you are already working too hard, or you are driven, or you are not being appreciated, so you may be a person who simply is showing up and operating at 50 percent or 60 percent. What we mean by a healthy work ethic is an attitude about our job, careers, and vocation, in which we really are there to make a difference and to make our signature known. After all, this is where we are spending our life, our hours, and our time. A healthy work ethic says, "I am accountable to God, I am accountable to my employers, I am accountable to my stockbrokers, I am accountable to my employees, I am accountable to the community, I am accountable to my spouse and my kids, to really show up not in body only, but to show up in spirit and attitude at 100 percent."

This may seem radical to a section of our work force that has an entitlement mentality, but when you are working, you are working. We are not e-mailing, we are not doing Internet shopping, we are not getting our personal things done on company time, but we are committed to the ethic of giving our best when we are on-site. Then, when we are off-site, we are able to disconnect and give our best as a family person, or a community person, or church person, whatever it may be. So a proper work ethic is not based on how many hours we work; it is a personal assessment about our ability to have the integrity that when no one is looking, our work ethic is the same.

I will never forget early in my development working during summers in high school as a groundskeeper. When my boss was not around I thought it was smart to be taking a nap---until the day he showed up unexpectedly while I was napping on the grass. It was a wake-up call for me that if I continued that kind of work ethic I would probably be a groundskeeper the rest of my life that would go from one project to another. Something happened to me that day and made me realize that if I was not to be trusted unless I was being supervised, I was not very intelligent vocationally. To be intelligent vocationally means to prepare ourselves, and then once we are on the job, to perspire ourselves and not be afraid to sweat, to expend energy, to give it our best.

The second spoke is what we are calling <u>service</u>. Service means that it is not about just our work ethic, our promotion, and us. It is about a contribution that we can make to help someone else be successful, to help a department be successful, and to have that kind of reputation where we are willing to help someone else get the credit. That can set us apart with the kind of intelligence a person has that is broader, wider, and bigger than someone simply coming in to want to have kudos for themselves. It requires perspiration because it means not only do we have to work, meet, and exceed the expectations on your own, but we need to go the extra mile and serve somebody intentionally; not grumbling, not complaining, not whining, but to actually do it with a sense of honoring another. Quite a different perspective than, "That is not part of my job description."

The next spoke under perspiration again is that foundational word <u>practice</u>. This time it is not elemental, but it is practice to be an <u>expert</u>. Reminding ourselves of the 10,000 hours theory can keep us from learning how to do something and then just coasting on autopilot or automatic. When we talk about vocational intelligence, we are talking about the kind of influence or impact that we can make. That requires you and I to perspire to a place of practice where we are really good at what we do. In other words, we are not just settling in for what is acceptable but we are targeting the exceptional. That requires practice, the willingness to try something and do it over and over again. Whether we are playing guitar or whether we are learning accounting, whether we are learning to dance or whether we are learning to present workshops, the ability to have a continual learning loop and practice towards those 10,000 hours is the mark of an intelligent person vocationally. A person who is a lifelong learner and is not satisfied by having a certain level of preparation, but is willing to practice and learn with feedback, this is the person who will embrace expert level practice.

The third area is <u>inspiration</u>. No matter what profession or career, calling or job, there needs to be a sense in which we are continually inspired by it. I was listening to a radio interview in which someone said, "I do not understand why I took this particular job. I really forgot what motivated me to it." Basically they were saying they were not happy and were not inspired themselves, and somehow lost the ability to have enough vocational intelligence to visit those places in their life that would keep them motivated and inspired to develop, grow, and to learn from their environment in their vocation.[106]

---

[106]See Robert Cooper, *The Other 90 Percent: How to Unlock Your Vast Untapped Potential for Leadership and Life* (New York: Three Rivers Press, 2001), chapters 13 and 24.

Inspiration begins with the first spoke of <u>personal development.</u> Personal development means we need to do the things that will cause us to grow. Get off the stuck, the starting block, and be able to accelerate. Some people may not like to read but in VQ the maxim "readers are leaders" holds some truth. However, we can learn to read not just books and literature, but people, environments, or even ourselves. We need to be able to get input or data from something, whether it is kinesthetic, bodily, whether it is visual, or whether it is books, literature, or conversations. However we "read" we need to read because we need new input to stretch us and new ways to think. I do not know of any better way to get on the program of personal development then to have your own tailor-made "reading" program. In other words, there are lots of tremendous things to listen to, see, read, and do, but all of them require a personal development plan (PDP) if they are going to seriously contribute to your personal development.[107]

We believe in coaching, especially with this series of transformational intelligences. By including the coaching piece and assessments you will be able to have a PDP that will help you have a track that works for you to accelerate your personal development, to keep you inspired, motivated, fanning the flames of the original fire that caused you to be excited, and looking forward to going to work.

---

[107]PDPs are personal because they are collaboratively designed with the unique person's context and competencies in mind. They are a development because they target and assess measurable growth in a specific area. They are plans because they have thought through checkpoints to measure where adjustments might need to be made along the way.

There is a great majority of 73 percent of people who are not happy where they work,[108] and I think it is their personal responsibility to keep themselves inspired and motivated by their own PDP. It cannot be a plan that is handed out by a supervisor. It is a plan that belongs to you, developed by you, but coached out of you by someone who is trained on how to do that and help you design something that is meaningful and motivating for you. So the first way to inspiration to increase your vocational intelligence is to have ongoing personal development built in regarding your job or career.

The second is <u>professional development</u>. Professional development involves not just things that cause you to grow personally, but things that cause you to develop professionally in what is expected of you in a particular career, job, or calling. Some people call these CEUs or continuing education units. Whatever we call them it is some of the recognized benchmarks in any vocation or profession, to continually upgrade ourselves and to allow ourselves to develop new ways of thinking, new input, latest technology, whatever it takes. I am so impressed with my chiropractor; he is always upgrading himself. Not only is he one of the most well-respected and beloved chiropractors in our area, but he has come up with ways to help me stay in the fight, stay in the game, because he is always assessing his professional development.

Now I believe in workshops and seminars for accomplishing this, but only when there is a plus on the other side. What do I mean by that? What I mean is many of us who leave our task during office hours to attend a

---

[108]Unpublished lecture notes from Dr. Bobby Hill and panel in the Vanguard Conference of Wylie, Texas, April 2007.

development workshop only come back to having to make up for the time we were away. We end up working twice as hard when we get back to catch up and by the time we get done getting back to where we were, we have forgotten pretty much what the workshop was all about and what was its intention apart from an interruption in our work flow. What we need is a plus where on the other side of a workshop we have some means of applying, integrating, and walking out some of the new concepts. I will rarely do a workshop or seminar without there being the plus of a debriefing conversation that could be had in a group, or with an individual, serving as a ninety-day "post seminar peer," or with a coach to ensure that we move from information to transformation, inculcating and integrating from the inside out.

The final spoke is called, again, <u>practice</u>. First, it is preparation, elemental practice, then in perspiration in terms of expert practice, and now we are saying to keep inspired we need to inspire others. That is level of practice that I call <u>instructional practice</u>. In other words, now we are helping others to practice the elements. Now we are helping others to practice at an expert level. We become a trainer, mentor, supervisor, some person who is able to teach, supervise, and help others. That will not only keep our skills sharp, but it will keep ourselves inspired with the satisfaction of knowing that we are passing on some of these things that we have learned, and begin enabling others to come behind us and be able to pick up where we left off. Passing the baton and leadership transition is a critical factor in any profession, calling, or job,[109] The ability for us to continue to make that

---

[109]See Collins, *Good to Great,* chapter two on level 5 leadership.

transition smoothly through our own teaching and supervision, our own modeling and mentoring, is critical.

Vocational intelligence is not just whatever a vocation needs in terms of minimal standards that are printed or published, but it is also the ability to prepare ourselves properly, to perspire ourselves continually, and to mostly inspire ourselves and others in key moments and in key ways. I want to give a "call to all" that will form these learning communities, these learning guilds. No one intends to climb Mount Everest on his or her own. We need to go with a team. We need Sherpa guides, coaches. We need people around us to go with us. I am calling all of you reading this not just to be intelligent individually, but also to be intelligent interdependently. VQ is about forming learning cultures, environments, and communities that coach each other, receive coaching, and receive the kind of ongoing help so that we can have the wealth of access and the wealth of influence while we are in the business of creating the wealth of dollars. Be willing to import this before you export it. As you apply these in your life and the lives of those you work with, as you engage a coach in the process or become a coach of this process to help others, I believe that you are going to see a difference in taking the "career mountains," and influencing the culture and the nation that these mountains impact. Thank you so much for being willing to be transformed and to be willing to discover how you are intelligent. Creating a culture of honor at home and work is your privilege and responsibility!

APPENDICES

7 mountains coaching
Excelling through Transformational Intelligences

"People must activate 'transformational intelligences' to impact their vocations in a lasting way. We have developed 7 mountains coaching as a key to peak performance along with peak significance. Before your feet hit the ground when you get out of bed in the morning, you will be looking forward to engaging the workplace with a perspective that will change everything about your day."

----Dr. Joseph Umidi, Life-forming Founder and President

Experience the coaching difference in your mountain: **Media, Business, Government, Education, Family, Religion, and Arts/Entertainment!**

Becoming a 7M "intel-agent" and/or a 7M coach adds to any leadership development strategy or training you are already using. Life-forming has proven materials that will enhance and accelerate your impact on the mountain you influence.

What's the Difference?
Vocational SignificanceValue-Based Performance Impact Your MountainTailor-made Transformation

7M is an opportunity for you, whatever mountain you are ascending in your nation, to experience the difference a coaching approach can make. It will help you:

•Move beyond career placement to vocational significance, satisfaction, and impact.

•Follow a proven system to fulfill your 7 mountains calling in a creative learning community process.

•Import and export a transformational change that is tailor-made for you and for those you work with.

•Enjoy the validation of receiving and applying value-based practices that go beyond standard career preparation.

What Are the Results?

There are results for the person being trained and for the person influenced by the trainee's vocational mountain. Those who go through this training can expect to:

•Experience sustainable peak performance in your vocation through assessments with coaching.

•Advance your impact and influence in your career calling through the 7 mountains transformational "intels."

•Train, coach, and lead others with tools that accelerate focus and materials that get results.

Register now at lifeformingcoach.com/7M

4Dcoaching

Tailor-Made Personal Development

Discover how to integrate the heart of a coach with the heart of God in transforming the heart of a disciple. This process will answer the questions: How do I know if I am a disciple? How do I know if I am making disciples?

Content (Instruction) + Context (Relationships, Life Experiences, and God Encounters) = Transformation

Discipleship coaching can be added to any discipleship strategy or curriculum you are already using. Through our proven materials Life-forming will help you accelerate your effectiveness in personally serving as a disciple to others.

Tailor-made discipleship

Unlock the Potential of Others!

Maximizing one-on-one culture with "First Steps" worldwide tested system.
Discover design with acclaimed Winslow Profile.
Assessment/Bible based.
Coach-based approach to discerning personal core values.
Activate God-given dreams for transformation.

4D taste and see.
4D self-study.
4D complete, w/coaching and assessments.

Design. Desire. Dreams. Destiny.

Register at lifeformingcoach.com/4D

Real Talk Training Seminar.

Life-forming Leadership Coaching will help you and your organization use professional coaching techniques to revolutionize your everyday communication. Unlock sustainable personal change through Real Talk Training:

- Connect relationally with your children.
- Communicate intimately with your spouse.
- Uncover forgotten dreams.
- Make conflict less damaging and more productive.
- Lead engaging meetings.
- Excel in customer service.
- About the Real Talk Training seminar.

Real Talk Training (RTT) is a one-day seminar, training leaders in effective interpersonal communication skills. RTT is an interactive experience, including demonstration, practice, and constructive feedback.

Drawing from the same insights and exercises of Life-forming Leadership Coaching's intensive programs, the RTT seminar equips attendees to use professional coaching techniques to revolutionize their everyday communications.

You also have the option to continue with the fifteen-week Accelerated Coach Training Program (ACT) at the end of the seminar.

The RTT seminar provides interactive training in listening for the deeper meaning, asking questions that open others up, and assisting them in solving problems permanently by *not* giving advice.

You'll learn ways to get a response instead of a reaction, how to jump-start a significant conversation with anyone, and how to avoid the number one killer of authentic communication.

Don't miss this opportunity to unlock sustainable change in your ability to communicate. The RTT seminar topics:

Session One: Real Talk Overview.

Session Two: Conversation Killers.

Session Three: Listening to What Really Matters.

Session Four: Ask More and Tell Less.

Session Five: Asking Powerful Questions.

Optional: ACT Workshop I Session.

Accelerated Coach Training Program (ACT)

A systematic and effective method to develop leaders with character and competence. Unlock sustainable change through the ACT Program:

- •Catalyze in-depth conversations.

- •Lead engaging meetings.

- •Listen intuitively.

- •Ask powerful questions.

- •Enhance your development of others.

The ACT Program is an in-depth, fifteen-week program designed for those who desire to use coaching practices in their current role. It employs a combination of two, one-day workshops, eight tele-class training sessions, and eight personal coaching sessions with a peer coach and/or coach trainer, to create personal transformation in the lives of the trainees.

Outcomes:

- •**Core values** – Deeply grasp the three core Life-forming coaching values and integrate them into your coaching and leadership practices.

•**Coaching defined** – Be able to define what coaching is, how it differs from mentoring and counseling, and then be able to develop and use basic coaching skills.

•**Intuitive listening** – Learn to listen with your intuition for the key words that can take the conversation to the transformational level.

•**Powerful questions** – Develop the skill of asking powerful questions which can open up new perspectives without causing a reaction.

•**Authenticity** – Experience an authentic peer relationship and develop the ability to catalyze authenticity with a coaching client.

•**Healthy accountability** – Experience healthy peer accountability, and demonstrate the ability to offer effective accountability to clients.

•**The G.R.O.W. model** – Become adept at using the G.R.O.W. model to focus a coaching conversation.

•**The coaching relationship** – Learn how to establish and structure a coaching relationship, then put that knowledge into practice with a coaching client.

•**Action steps** – Learn how to develop clear and challenging action steps with a high level of buy-in from the client.

•**Expectations** – Be able to maintain expectations and momentum in a coaching relationship.

Professional Coach Training

Unlock sustainable personal change through the professional program:

- Develop a strategic growth plan for your clients.

- Craft life purpose statements for yourself and your clients.

- Make conflict less damaging and more productive.

- Catalyze in-depth conversations.

- Listen intuitively.

- Ask powerful questions.

- Reflect and distill principles for anchoring sustainable growth

The professional program is a one-year training program created to prepare you for coaching at the professional level. The program is composed of three tracks: formation, life focus, and implementation. Each track is thirteen to fourteen weeks in length.

Professional Leadership Coach Qualification.
Earn a highly respected qualification and join the worldwide coaching movement as a professional coach.

Formation Track.
Practice the values, techniques, and relational skills needed to coach personal change, including accountability, feedback, learning from life, and building growth-centered relationships.

Life Focus Track.
Define your personal life purpose using tangible tools. The track encompasses dreaming, goal-setting, personal values, life purpose, and biblical life planning. Completion of formation or ACT upgrade is required.

Implementation Track.
Advanced coaching skills and exercises, including practical tools for identifying and engaging growth issues in others. You will learn to create growth plans for almost any coaching issue. Completion of life focus is required.

Life-forming Executive Consulting

"Character-Based" Human Capital Solutions

During these challenging economic times, organizations are searching for viable business solutions that can help streamline their operational efficiencies, mitigate their risks, reduce unnecessary expenditures, and a process to empower their human capital assets (people). Organizations continue to be concerned about hiring, developing, and retaining the right people with not only the right job skills, but more importantly, the right people with good character and behavior that are aligned with their overall culture, mission, and business objectives.

Life-forming Leadership Coaching appreciates the opportunity to share with you human capital technologies and solutions that can provide you with a tremendous value proposition to share with your clients. A person's character and behavior have become such major factors regarding human capital decision making (i.e., talent acquisitions, employee development, and succession planning) that organizations are realizing they must incorporate "objective processes" to help make better, "more predictable" human capital decisions.

This can be accomplished by implementing valuable processes that help to:

- Align people to an organization's culture.
- Define performance requirements per hiring position.

•Assess a person's character and behavior (beyond just job skills / experience).

•Provide an ongoing learning environment that enhances performance and productivity.

For more details and free downloads see:
http://lifeformingcoach.com/executive_consulting

Sample Coaching Plan

Name: Jerry Jones: Overcoming anger. **Hours/Week**: Two - three hours/week.

Growth goal: To cut the number of times I have angry outbursts at work over the next three months in half, and identify and deal with some of the roots of it.

Appointment 1
Date:

✿ Review progress (Note: growth goal was set during intake process).

✿ Discuss causes of anger and how to raise awareness of it.

✿ Review the coaching plan, finalize, and get buy-in for doing it.

Action steps:
✿ Journal on three recent incidents where you got angry.

✿ Find and start a book on anger; note three key learnings.

✿ Find a peer who can provide SEA (support, accountability, and encouragement) for you.

Appointment 2
Date:
✿ Review progress; discuss insights from action steps.

❀ Discuss, "In what situations do I get angry?" Look at root

❀ Is peer relationship in place?

Action steps:

❀ When you get upset this week, affirm or compliment the person instead.

❀ Continue study on anger from last week; note three more key insights.

❀ Set up accountability plan with peer (three times per week).

Appointment 3
Date:

❀ Review progress; check in on peer accountability and SEA.

❀ Discuss impact of moving in opposite reaction (affirming vs. venting).

❀ Identify what is working and what is needed for long-term change.

Action steps:

❀ Continue accountability plan and SEA with peer.

❀ Continue to do something positive to affirm another each time you get angry.

❀ Identify stress points that upset you; eliminate one each week.

Resource Index

Multiple Intelligence Theory

Armstrong, T. *You're Smarter than You Think: A Kid's Guide to Multiple Intelligences.* Minneapolis: Free Spirit, 2003.

Kagan, S., and M. Kagan. *Multiple Intelligences: The Complete MI Book.* Kagan Publishing, 2002.

Gardner, Howard, *Multiple Intelligences.* New York: Basic Books, 2006.

Coaching

Logan, David, and John King. *The Coaching Revolution.* Avon, MA: Adams Media Corporation, 2001.

Lombardo, Michael M., and Robert W. Eichinger. *For Your Information: A Development and Coaching Guide*: Lominger Limited, 1996.

Morgan, Howard et al., eds. *Profiles in Coaching: The 2004 Handbook of Best Practices in Leadership Coaching.* 2003.

Stephenson, Peter. *Executive Coaching.* Nella Soeterboek, 2000.

Whitmore, John. *Coaching for Performance.* Brealey Publishing, 1996.

Spiritual Wheel

Bowell, Richard. *The Seven Steps of Spiritual Intelligence: The Practical Pursuit of Purpose, Success and Happiness.* Brealey Publishing, 2005.

Brown, Carol A. *The Mystery of Spiritual Sensitivity: Your Practical Guide to Responding to Burdens You Feel from God's Heart.* Destiny Image Publishers, 2008.

Gowen, Dennis Jeanne. *Running Barefoot on Holy Ground: Childlike Intimacy with God.* Kregel Publications, 2006.

Pava, Moses L., and Patrick Primaeaux. *Spiritual Intelligence at Work: Meaning, Metaphor, and Morals.* Emerald Group Publishing, 2003.

Emotional Wheel

Cooper, Cary. *Organizational Stress Management: A Strategic Approach.* Palgrave McMillan, 2010.

Jawer, Michael, and Mark S. Micozzi. *The Spiritual Anatomy of Emotion: How Feelings Link the Brain, the Body, and the Sixth Sense.* Inner Traditions International, 2009.

Maxwell, John C. *Teamwork 101: What Every Leader Needs to Know.* Thomas Nelson, 2009.

Stein, Steven, et al. *Emotional Intelligence Skills Assessment.* John Wiley & Sons, 2009.

Wellness Wheel

Dodd, Pamela, and Doug Sundheim. *The 25 Best Time Management Tools and Techniques: How to Get More Done Without Driving Yourself Crazy.* Peak Performance Press, 2008.

Hafer, Tom P. *Faith and Fitness: Diet and Exercise for a Better World.* Augsburg Books, 2006.

Loehr, Jim, and Tony Schwartz. *The Power of Full Engagement: Managing Energy, Not Time, Is the Key to High Performance and Personal Renewal.* New York: Simon & Schuster, 2004.

Sraya, Yehonatan. *A Guide to Better Health: A Holistic Approach.* Simcha Media Group, 2005.

Financial Wheel

Alcorn, Randy C. *Money, Possessions, and Eternity.* Tyndale House Publishers, 2003.

Gold, Jacob H. *Financial Intelligence: Getting Back to Basics after an Economic Meltdown.* Cambridge House Media, 2009.

Pennells, Sarah. *How to Save and Invest Ethically.* A & C Black, 2009.

Schervish, Paul G. *Wealth and the Will of God: Discerning the Use of Riches in the Service of Ultimate Purpose.* Indiana University Press, 2010.

Smith, Pueges Deborah. *Financial Survival in Uncertain Times: Prioritize Your Spending - Master Your Debt - Secure Your Future - Maintain Your Peace of Mind.* Harvest House Publishers, 2009.

Culture Wheel

Copeland, Germai. *Prayers that Avail Much for Leaders.* Harrison House, 2009.

Ford, Leighton. *The Attentive Life: Discerning God's Presence in All Things.* InterVarsity Press, 2008.

Maxwell, John C. *Talent Is Never Enough: Discover the Choices That Will Take You Beyond Your Talent.* Thomas Nelson, 2007.

Relational Wheel

169

Grimshaw, Jeff. *Leadership Without Excuses: How to Create Accountability and High Performance.* New York: McGraw-Hill, 2010.

Johnson, Craig Edward. *Meeting the Ethical Challenges of Leadership: Casting Light or Shadow.* Sage Publications, 2008.

Vocational Wheel

Hennings, Chad. *Rules of Engagement: Finding Friendship, Faith, and Strength in a Disconnected World.* FaithWords, 2010.

Bibliography

Books

Allen, Robert. *Multiple Streams of Income: How Ordinary People Make Extraordinary Money Online*: John Wiley & Sons, 2006.

Clinton, Robert, and Paul Stanley. *Connecting: The Mentoring Relationships You Need to Succeed*. NavPress Publishing Group, 1992.

Clinton, Robert. *The Making of a Leader: Recognizing the Lessons and Stages of Leadership Development*. NavPress Publishing Group, 1988.

Collins, Jim. *Good to Great*: HarperCollins Publishing, 2001.

Cooper, Robert K. *The Other 90 Percent: How to Unlock Your Vast Untapped Potential for Leadership and Life*: Three Rivers Press, 2001.

Cordeiro, Wayne and Robert Lewis. *Culture Shift: Transforming Your Church from the Inside Out*: John Wiley & Sons, 2005.

Cunningham, Loren. *Is that You God?: Hearing the Voice of God*. Y.W.A.M. Publishing, 2002.

Gardner, Howard. *The Theory of Multiple Intelligences*. Academic Internet Publishing, 2006.

Gladwell, Malcolm. *Outliers: The Story of Success*. Little, Brown, and Company, 2008.

Kiyosaki, Robert. *Increase Your Financial IQ*: Business Plus, 2008.

Loehr, Jim and Tony Schwartz. *The Power of Full Engagement: Managing Energy, Not Time, Is the Key to High Performance and Personal Renewal*. New York: Simon & Schuster, 2004.

Malphurs, Audrey. *Values-Driven Leadership: Discovering and Developing Your Core Values for Ministry.* Baker Books, 2004.

Maxwell, John C. *Failing Forward: Turning Mistakes into Stepping Stones for Success.* Thomas Nelson, 2007.

Robinson, Ken. *The Element: How Finding Your Passion Changes Everything.* Penguin Group, 2009.

Scott, Susan. *Fierce Conversations: Achieving Success at Work and in Life One Conversation at a Time.* Penguin Group, 2004.

Swenson, Richard. *Margin: Restoring Emotional, Physical, Financial, and Time Reserves to Overloaded Lives.* NavPress Publishing Group, 2004.

_____ *The Overload Syndrome.* NavPress Publishing Group, 2004.

Zohr, Danah and Ian Marshall. *Spiritual Quotient: Connecting with Our Spiritual Intelligence.* Bloomsbury, 2001.

Goleman, Daniel, Richard Boyatzis, and Annie McKee. *Primal Leadership: Realizing the Power of Emotional Intelligence.* Cambridge: Harvard Business School Publishing, 2002.

Berkman, Lisa et al. "Emotional Support and Survival after Myocardial Infarction," *Annals of Internal Medicine* Insert Publisher,1992.

Umidi, Joseph. *Transformational Coaching: Bridge Building that Impacts, Connects, and Advances the Ministry and the Marketplace.* Xulon Press, 2005.

Dissertations
Pescosolido, Anthony T. "Emotional Intensity in Groups." PhD diss., Case Western Reserve University, 2000.

Web sites

www.fda.govwww.lancelearning.com
www.lifeformingcoach.com
www.mayoclinic.com/health/exercise/HQ01676
www.theaterchurch.com
www.thecoachingpair.com
www.u1stfinancial.net/equityforming

About the Author

Dr. Joseph Umidi has authored four books and numerous training manuals in his 28 years of graduate school teaching, and in the 24 country training centers he has established in thirteen languages with his award winning Lifeforming Leadership Coaching curriculum. Sought out as an Executive Coach and Organizational Trainer, this book is a response to meet the challenges and opportunities that he has gleaned in both his research and professional practice in the marketplace.

Joseph serves as professor at Regent University for the past twenty-eight years focusing on Transformational Leadership Development. He is the founder and president of Lifeforming Leadership Coaching, Inc. Over the last fifteen years he established an award-winning curriculum to transform leaders and their organizational cultures in business, government, education, and non-profits that is now being used in numerous schools and organizations.

Joseph is married to Marie, founder and president of TMCJ, Inc., an international arts organization, and they are the delighted grandparents of three grandchildren. They reside in Virginia Beach, Virginia.

Recent Training Summary
* Millennium-Copthorne Hotel Group for culture shift for customer-service excellence with 450 managers and 4700 employees.
*Stefano Construction Organization for creative approaches to team building with 6 U.S. centers.

*Virginia State government workers for Community Transformation training curriculum with 14 community partners and two universities.

*South African government leaders for leadership mentoring for HIV-Aids prevention

*World-Vision international for organizational values alignment and innovation

*Department of Education for Superintendent Management excellence in Singapore

Websites
www.7mcoaching.com
www.merittrainingcorp.com

Made in the USA
San Bernardino, CA
29 January 2014